Product Innovation Strategy Pure and Simple

Other McGraw-Hill Books by Michel Robert

STRATEGY PURE AND SIMPLE: HOW WINNING CEOs OUTTHINK THEIR COMPETITION

Product Innovation Strategy Pure and Simple

How Winning Companies Outpace Their Competitors

Michel (Mike) Robert

McGraw-Hill, Inc.

New York   San Francisco   Washington, D.C.   Auckland   Bogotá
Caracas   Lisbon   London   Madrid   Mexico City   Milan
Montreal   New Delhi   San Juan   Singapore
Sydney   Tokyo   Toronto

Library of Congress Cataloging-in-Publication Data

Robert, Michel.
  Product innovation strategy pure and simple : how winning
companies outpace their competitors / Michel Robert.
      p.   cm.
  Includes index.
  ISBN 0-07-053132-3
  1. New products—Management.   I. Title.
HF5415.153.R63   1995
658.5'75—dc20   95-11855
                                                           CIP

1 2 3 4 5 6 7 8 9 0   DOC/DOC   9 0 0 9 8 7 6 5

ISBN 0-07-053132-3

*The sponsoring editor for this book was Betsy Brown, the editing supervisor
was Jane Palmieri, and the production supervisor was Pamela Pelton. It was
set in Palatino by Victoria Khavkina of McGraw-Hill's Professional Book
Group composition unit.*

Printed and bound by R. R. Donnelley & Sons Company.

*To my wife Ellie, my best critic, for enduring
my writing books on our honeymoon and
our vacations. And to my daughters, Emma
and Samantha, whom I hope will be
inspired to realize that achievement in life
is totally unrelated to one's origin.*

Contents

14. The Tangible and Intangible Outputs of the Process   165

Foreword

In 1989 and 1990, as we struggled to restructure our company, I and other Caterpillar managers spent many hours locked up in a room with Mike Robert talking about strategy and product innovation. Mike told us many things we didn't like to hear, but they were instrumental in our restructuring process.

In his latest book, *Product Innovation Strategy*, Mike has some nice things to say about Caterpillar. We appreciate that. I think we're better at product innovation today, so perhaps we deserve some of the compliments. If Caterpillar is indeed better, it is certainly due in part to our work with Mike.

I think anyone interested in product innovation (and who isn't?) will benefit from reading Mike's latest writing on the subject—just as Caterpillar has benefited from his knowledge.

Don Fites
Chairman and Chief Executive Officer
Caterpillar, Inc.

Preface

Back in the early 1960s, when I was working for Johnson & Johnson, I noticed that we, as a company, had the ability to introduce new products successfully at a much faster pace than our competitors. That thought intrigued me long after I left the company.

My interest in this area was provoked again in the 1980s during my consulting work with dozens of 3M divisions around our strategic thinking process. Once more, I came across a company that had the ability to conceive and introduce hundreds of new products annually without much of a competitive response.

The same experience was repeated when we started to work with Caterpillar. Again I encountered a company that had the ability, over the decades, to create and introduce an ongoing stream of new products at a pace no competitor could match.

Then came the Japanese and companies like Sony and Honda, which had developed the identical capability.

These three events finally caused me, in the mid-1980s, to start investigating how these companies were able to consistently outpace their competitors in the area of new product creation and introduction. Fortunately, because of our strategy work, we already had access to dozens of companies with this capability, which provided us with the best laboratory in the world—real organizations.

We then set out to study these organizations in an attempt to uncover the process they had perfected. As a result, what you will find in this book is not a "miracle recipe" pulled out of the sky but, rather, concepts and a process that were extracted out of the heads of real people running real organizations while they were in the throes of creating and introducing new products and creating markets.

All we, at DPI, have done is to codify these concepts and build instruments around them that enable an organization to accelerate its product creation manyfold.

I hope you enjoy the process and I wish you . . .

Good reading!

Michel (Mike) Robert

1

New Product Creation: The Corporate Fountain of Youth

There was a time, not so long ago, that one could walk into any office anywhere in the world, from Prudential Insurance to Siemens to General Motors to AT&T to Michelin Tires, and see hundreds of Friden calculators on row after row of wooden desks.

There was a time, not so long ago, that one could go into any office anywhere in the world and see several duplicating machines made by Addressograph Multigraph.

There was a time, not so long ago, that one could walk into any store in the world, large or small, and see one cash register, if not several, made by the National Cash Register Company.

There was a time, not so long ago, when one could go into any house in the United States, and some other one hundred countries, and find a Singer sewing machine.

There was a time, not so long ago, when these four companies—Singer, Adressograph Multigraph, NCR, and Friden—were industrial powerhouses with worldwide brand recognition. However, just a few years later, two of these companies are almost extinct, and the other two do not command the market presence they once did.

There was a time, not so long ago, when another group of companies had very dominant market positions, and, somehow, they have been able to maintain and even enhance their positions. These are companies such as 3M, Caterpillar, Coca-Cola, Johnson & Johnson, Merck, Marks & Spencer, Castrol, Hewlett-Packard, and Rubbermaid, to name but a few.

In every country, in every industry, one can identify two distinct types of companies: those that seem to have an ability to perpetuate themselves over long periods and those that do not. Once this discovery is made, one needs to then ask, as we did: "What is it that companies with the ability to perpetuate themselves know about business that the others either don't know or have forgotten about?"

The answer to this question, in our view, is the solution to the corporate fountain of youth. In our opinion, the companies which can maintain, and even enhance, their market positions over time have mastered the process of strategic product creation and innovation.

The Process of Strategic Product Creation and Innovation

Without continuous product innovation, organizations sputter and die. Every sane business executive will attest to this hypothesis. Not so long ago one of the most revered names in the bicycle industry was Schwinn, the 97-year-old company based in Chicago. Yet, in 1992, Schwinn declared bankruptcy. With the advent of a multitude of new bicycle designs in the 1970s and 1980s, Schwinn failed to see the changes sweeping the industry. According to *Forbes*, "Schwinn was obsessed with cutting costs, instead of innovation." Nonetheless, most organizations practice product innovation in a haphazard manner, apparently hoping that it will happen. In a DPI survey of 200 *Fortune* 500 companies, two-thirds said they had no formal manner by which to encourage the search for and the development of new products, customers, or markets.

The United States's innovative prowess has eroded in the last two decades. However, some U.S. corporations are still among the world's best. Caterpillar, Merck, 3M, Johnson & Johnson, Hewlett-Packard, Intel, Pepsico, Rubbermaid, Procter & Gamble, and some others seem to have an infinite ability to churn out new products at a dizzying speed, which means that the skill is alive and well. In fact, in these companies product innovation is viewed as a paranoiac need. These organizations consider their abilities to continuously find opportunities for new products and markets and to develop better and faster processes to manufacture and deliver them as their "lifeline."

Why then, do some firms grow and prosper while others deteriorate and decline?

The answer, we believe, lies in the ability to manage *change*. Furthermore, the prosperous organizations have also developed a *process* to manage change on an ongoing basis in order to generate a constant stream of new product and market concepts.

It is our contention that there is a *systematic process* to product creation and introduction and that in long-lived organizations such a process is being practiced consciously, whereas less successful organizations think it is a "chance" happening.

Change: The Fuel of Corporate Longevity

Before discussing the process of product creation, one needs to understand the role of *change* in this process. Change is the *raw material* of product innovation. One cannot have product innovation without change. There is a direct linear extrapolation between the amount of change found in an organization's business environment and the amount of new product opportunities uncovered. The more change, the more room for new product creation; the less change present, the less new product innovation. In fact, new product innovation *thrives on change!*

As a consequence, innovative companies also thrive on change. Innovative companies do not see change as bad but rather as a constant source of new product or market opportunity. The attitude that change is healthy is a key difference between winners and losers, leaders and followers. Seeing change as healthy is a critical mind-set that the CEO of any company must instill throughout the organization to guarantee long-term survival.

One CEO who clearly understands this concept is Christopher Sinclair of PepsiCo Foods & Beverages International who says: "You want an organization out there that's passionate about change" ("Pepsi Opens a Second Front," *Fortune*, August 8, 1994). Even *Fortune* magazine, in an August 8, 1994, article entitled "Lessons from America's Fastest Growing Companies," comes to an identical conclusion: "Entrepreneurs thrive by sowing fields—industries, eras—plowed by *change*. The present, with the landscape tossed up by a fundamental economic transformation, affords wonderful opportunities."

Another company, however, that has not had an overriding passion for change is Borden, the creator of condensed milk. After having built a preeminent position in ice cream, cheese, and milk and having made Elsie the world's best-known cow, Borden diversified into a wide array of other consumer-oriented products such as Wise potato chips, Prince's spaghetti, and Classico tomato sauce. All these products, when acquired, had dominant positions of their own. Today, they are remnants of their former selves. The reason is simple. Borden, under a succession of CEOs, demonstrated an inability to cope with change. In the ice cream business, it sat idly by as the market changed and migrated toward super-premium brands such as Ben & Jerry's, Breyer's, Baskin Robbins, Häagen Dazs and others. Borden's ice cream retails for 40 percent less than these newer products and has lost considerable market share. The same is true of its newer acquisitions. In the spaghetti business, Borden missed the trend toward the quick-preparation alternatives and was surpassed by new entries such as Rice-a-Roni's, which retail for 80 percent more. The same is true for chips, where the company did not notice the trend toward "ethnic" chips such as tortilla chips introduced by Frito-Lay, which also sell for a 40% premium over Borden's. As a result of this tremendous inability to recognize and cope with change, Borden today is on the verge of bankruptcy and has just been taken over by corporate raider Kravis, Kolberg & Roberts, which will surely dismantle Borden and sell off the pieces.

Change, as the root of new product creation, is a fundamental concept of innovation. Consequently, assessing changes that can affect an organization must be part of a deliberate process that can then convert these changes into concepts for new products, services, customers, and/or markets. Furthermore, this process must do more than just create new concepts. It must also ensure the successful introduction of such new products.

New Product Creation as a Repeatable Business Practice

If one cannot codify a skill or talent, one cannot make it a repeatable business practice. In less successful organizations, product creation is often seen as a solitary undertaking or the responsibility of a few "brilliant" people that, as such, totally depends on boldness, creativity, or flashes of genius. Our experience shows that product innovation is a *deliberate process* and is viewed as such by long-lived, successful companies. As such, product innovation is an organizational skill that has been codified so that it has become a *repeatable business practice* known and used by everyone in the company. Moreover, product innovation is an offensive weapon much more than a defensive one. Henry Ford, one of the great product innovators, said: "It could almost be written down as a formula that when a man begins to think that he at last has found the method, he had better begin a most searching examination of himself to see whether some part of his brain has not gone to sleep." Product creation, in other words, needs to be a constant process. Too many organizations "go to sleep" after one or two "hits." The key to success is to have a deliberate process that can be made into a *continuous and repeatable business practice.*

The Different Forms of Innovation

Innovation is a much misunderstood word. To some it means technological breakthroughs, whereas to others it means something akin to the "big bang" theory of the universe.

For the purpose of outlining a process of innovative thinking, we will attempt to describe the different forms that innovation can take. The first distinction that needs to be made is between *innovation* and *invention.* Innovation is the broader concept of continuous improvement, whereas invention is one form of innovation. Inventions are usually associated with discoveries—technology, patents, formulas, and so forth. Inventions can lead to major breakthroughs. There are however, many other forms of innovation that are more mundane but that, over time, can give an organization a sustainable competitive advantage. We will discuss these other forms in the following chapters. There are two areas of an organization in which innovation or invention can occur. The first is in the development of new products and/or the improvement of current ones, usually referred to as *product* innovation. The second is in the improvement of the processes that sell, manufacture, deliver, or service the products, usually referred to as *process* innovation.

In each of these two areas, we will build a case to demonstrate that the best companies do not believe in big bang innovation but rather in the more mundane approach of marginal, incremental, but continuous innovation to the organization's products and processes.

If you believe in the big bang approach to innovation—namely invention—it will be a long time between bangs. One industry that practices this approach is the pharmaceutical industry, in which a new prescription product comes along every dozen years or so. In contrast, 3M had hundreds of different versions of its Post-it note pads within months of producing its original yellow, finger-size format. Each additional version was only a marginal, incremental improvement over the previous one. Nonetheless, it is this ability to continuously innovate that gives 3M an edge over its competitors. No other competitor has been able to keep pace with this extraordinary skill.

Strong product-creation companies do not count on home runs or the big bang approach to innovation. If they do come across big bang ideas, all the better. In the meantime, however, these companies believe in and practice continuous, marginal, incremental innovation in every aspect of the business and on the part of everyone in the organization.

In an article entitled "Tough-Minded Ways to Get Innovative" (*Harvard Business Review*, May/June 1988), Andrall E. Pearson talked about innovation at Hasbro, one of the most successful and innovative toy companies. He said:

> Unlike most of its competitors, Hasbro doesn't focus on inventing new blockbuster toys. Its management will take blockbusters, if they come along, of course. But the company doesn't spend the bulk of its product development dollars on such long-odds bets. Instead, it centers its efforts on staple-toy lines like G.I. Joe, Transformers, games and preschool basics that can be extended and renewed each year.

It is no accident that 3M and Rubbermaid introduce over 300 new products per year, that Merck has introduced 12 new "block buster" drugs in 10 years and that 90 percent of Rubbermaid's new products are successful—numbers that are mind-boggling to most so-called experts. The secret? A deliberate process that *causes* new product creation to occur. One of the primary tasks of the CEO therefore, if the organization is to perpetuate itself, is to install a deliberate process of systematic innovation and provide management mechanisms that ensure its practice on a continuous basis by everyone in the organization.

Key Definitions

Before we look at the process of new product creation and introduction, it might be useful to introduce some key definitions that are at the root of our process:

- Entrepreneurial, innovative organizations are those that are constantly looking to *redeploy assets and resources from areas of low yield and low productivity to areas of higher yield and higher productivity.*

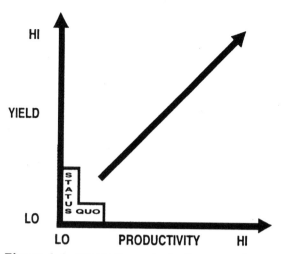

Figure 1-1. Innovative organizations are always looking to redeploy assets and resources from low yield and low productivity to higher yield and higher productivity.

- Product innovation is the *tool* used by these organizations and, as such, it is the *process of systematically anticipating, recognizing, and exploiting change.*
- *Change is the raw material* of new product innovation.

The following chapters will take you through each step of this process, and the last chapter will discuss methods that can be employed to institutionalize this process in an organization.

The Process of Product Innovation

The product innovation process has four distinct steps, as shown in Figure 1-2.

Figure 1-2. Four steps of the product innovation process.

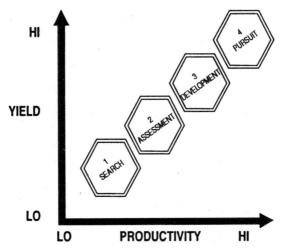

Figure 1-3. Using the product innovation process to redeploy assets to areas of higher yield and productivity.

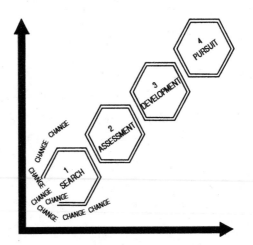

Figure 1-4. Change is the raw material of product innovation.

1. *Search.* Innovative organizations know where to look in their environment for changes that can be converted into opportunities for new products, customers, or markets.

2. *Assessment.* Innovative organizations know how to assess opportunities against four key criteria to rank opportunities in terms of their overall potential.

3. *Development.* Innovative organizations can anticipate the critical factors that will lead to the success or failure of each opportunity.

4. *Pursuit.* Innovative organizations can develop an implementation plan that promotes success and avoids failure.

This is the process that allows the redeployment of assets and resources from areas of low yield and low productivity to areas of higher yield and higher productivity (Figure 1-3).

And *change* is the raw material of that process (Figure 1-4).

2

The Seven Deadly Sins of Corporate Stagnation

Why is it that 3M kicks out between 300 and 500 new products per year and has been doing so for many years without interruption? Why is it that Johnson & Johnson can continuously bring a stream of new health care products to market in an industry that is so-called regulated? Why is it that Merck can introduce new prescription drugs at a pace six times that of its competitors? Why is it that Rubbermaid can introduce new products with a success rate that is higher than 90 percent with no market testing, when experts tell us that 90 percent of all new products fail? Why is it that Intel can bang out new PC chips faster than PC manufacturers can assemble them? Why is it that Caterpillar can introduce unique new earth-moving machines with features, and at a rate, that no one else can match?

Why is it that these companies, and a few others, can create and introduce a continuous flow of new products but their competitors cannot?

This is a question that has intrigued this author for the last 30 years. Finally, 10 years ago, I set out to find an answer. The approach was simple. Go and talk to these firms and have them explain to me how they do it. However, none of them could, because whatever process they had developed, they were practicing by *osmosis*. As a result, anything that cannot be codified cannot be explained rationally nor can it be transferred. As such, the skill is attributed to all sorts of irrelevant phenomena.

Part of our research, however, consisted also of visits with companies that were generally viewed as not being on the cutting edge of new product innovation in an attempt to understand why they seemed to lack this skill. What we discovered were a series of self-imposed impediments that caused them to lag behind and, in some cases, lead them to extinction.

"We must protect our cash cow at all costs, or else we perish."

Every company has a product or a market that is its cash cow. *Never worship at the altar of the cash cow.* You will inevitably perish. The reasoning is simple. For every employee that you train in techniques to protect your cash cow, there are 1000 people in competitive organizations thinking of ways to destroy your cash cow. And the odds are that they eventually will succeed.

IBM is a case in point. IBM's cash cow, as we all know, has been its mainframes—once the powerhouses of computing capacity. Over the years IBM has done everything in its power to protect that cash cow. Unfortunately, with the advent of smarter chips from companies such as Intel, Motorola, Fujitsu, and Advanced Microdevices together with the development of smaller and smaller computers with increasing capacity by such companies as Apple, Compaq, Dell, AST, and Gateway, the mainframe's importance has been on a downward spiral for the last 10 years, and so has IBM's economic performance.

The unfortunate element in this cruel scenario is that the first PC chip—RISC—was developed by IBM—in 1973! To this day, it is a chip more powerful than anything brought to market by anyone else. IBM made a deliberate decision not to introduce this chip because the company could foresee the devastating effects it would have on its mainframe business. In 1994, 21 years later and maybe 21 years too late, IBM has finally introduced it under the brand name PowerPC.

Another company, however, that has been thriving from these same changes is Hewlett-Packard. During this same period, HP has gone from seventh in the industry to second, and its stock has zoomed from $40 to over $90. Why? The reason is simple. In the words of its CEO, Lewis Platt: "The best defense," Platt says, "is preemptive self-destruction and renewal. We have to be willing to cannibalize what we're doing today in order to ensure our leadership in the future. It's counter to human nature, but you have to kill your business while it is still working" ("How HP Continues to Grow and Grow," *Fortune*, May 2, 1994).

Once a company starts worshipping at the altar of the cash cow, its decision-making process becomes paralyzed. Once paralyzed, no new initiatives are undertaken in the debilitating interest of protecting the cash cow.

"Our industry is mature; there is no more growth or innovation possible."

Some people would claim that the reason products become generic, prices come down to the lowest level, and growth stops is that the "market is mature." Mature markets, in our view, are a myth.

Consider some examples. Who would have thought 10 years ago that people would pay $300 for a pair of shoes? Running shoes at that! After all, everyone had a pair, and the market was mature. Then along came Nike and Reebok!

Who would have thought 10 years ago that people would be paying $3000 for a bicycle? After all, everyone had one, and the market was mature. Then along came Shimano and its "mountain" bikes with 21 speeds!

In yet another business, the former management of A. E. Staley thought that the corn milling business was mature and decided to embark on a diversification spree to become a consumer products marketer that nearly destroyed the company. Its new owners, Tate & Lyle, decided to rededicate the company to its previous core business with great success. Its CEO, Neil Shaw, told *Forbes* in an interview "The old management took their eyes off the ball. We got back to doing what we do best—we're corn millers." With its old strategy back in vogue, Staley introduced new products, one of which is a fat substitute made from corn that has reversed the firm's financial performance overnight and put it back on a highly profitable road.

Adolph Coors is another company that has managed to grow impressively in the beer business—an industry considered by Busch and Miller to be mature. This was achieved by introducing an avalanche of new products aimed at niche markets. Furthermore, while the large breweries are cannabalizing each other's markets to maintain their share and volume, a host of "micro" breweries have emerged to give birth to new, niche brands such as Samuel Adams, Sharps, and O'Douls. While the big breweries see the market as mature and have stopped innovating, the only growth in the U.S. market is coming from these innovative, micro breweries which are thriving. Ten years ago, there were only a few; today, there are over 500!

Even in the liquor industry, probably one of the world's most mature industries, that concept is a myth—not decided by us, but by the CEO of one of the industry's most successful players. In a market where consumption is dropping 1 percent per year on a worldwide basis, the CEO of Guinness argues, as reported in the November 4, 1991, issue of *Fortune:* "Consumption is not actually a very good indicator in any business of whether there are any opportunities there." To prove his point, CEO Anthony Tennant defers to his company's performance—$1.2 billion of earnings on sales of $3.8 billion for an operating profit margin of 31 percent. Furthermore, all four of the major players in this field produced margins of over 25 percent. So much for mature markets.

The military truck industry is yet another market which most truck manufacturers view as mature and, as a result, hasn't seen any changes in truck design since the Korean war—45 years ago. That is, until Stewart & Stevenson, based in Houston, looked at the business and decided to do something about it. They have developed a new truck that can consistently outclimb its rivals on dirt as well as sand because of a system that automatically inflates and deflates the truck's tires to give the vehicle more surface tension on slippery or rough terrain. As a result, Stewart & Stevenson, unknown in the industry a few years ago, has won contracts for over 20,000 trucks against formidable competitors such as Volvo, General Motors, and Mercedes.

In yet another so-called mature industry—that of commercial buildings—one company has found growth. Honeywell, the manufacturer of temperature control devices, has found a new growth path. By combining its control technology with that of sensors, it has introduced a new product which controls lights, security, and temperature and shuts off the television and closes the windows. Michael Bonsignore, Honeywell's CEO, states: "And somebody says there's no growth in building. We just have to know where to look."

Ultimate proof that there is no such thing as a mature business or industry may be a recent study done by David Birch of Cognetics, a Cambridge, Massachusetts, research company. His study attempted to identify America's fastest-growing companies. These companies, referred to as "gazelles" by Birch, are companies that have doubled in size every year from $100,000 in revenues in 1989. The results are revealing. The industries with the most fast-growing gazelles tend to be the aged and moribund. In fact, there seems to be an inverse relationship between an industry's health and the concentration of gazelles. Of the 20 gazelle-friendliest industries, not one was in the top 20 in terms of growth (see Table 2-1).

Table 2-1. Industries with Fast-Growth Companies*

Industry	Percent of companies that are fast growers
Paper products	8.3
Chemicals	7.8
Instruments	7.7
Rubber, plastics	7.6
Electric & electronic equipment	7.2
Banking	7.0
Insurance carriers	6.8
Food products	6.4
Primary metal products	6.2
Wholesale trade (nondurables)	6.2

*Industries with the largest share of companies that at least doubled revenues between 1989 and 1993 from a minimum of $100,000.

The concept of a mature market, in our view, resides in the mind of the beholder. In other words, it is a state of mind. Management convinces itself that its business is mature, and, as a result, two things start to happen: First, the company stops looking for opportunities because it has convinced itself there are no more. Therefore, it stops innovating. Second, the company starts diverting its resources to unrelated opportunities that take it way off course, usually with disastrous results.

There are always opportunities, particularly if one is practicing market fragmentation! As D. Wayne Calloway, the CEO of Pepsico, a company that is viewed as being in a mature industry but is outpacing its competitors in growth, puts it in a *Fortune* article: "If the market you're in isn't growing, you'd better find a way to make it grow" ("Lessons from America's Fastest Growing Companies," August 8, 1994).

"We're in a commodity business."

Another self-fulfilling prophecy. There is no such thing as a commodity business. There is always the possibility of differentiating yourself. Commodity businesses are a state of mind as well. Your company's products become commodities when management convinces itself that they are.

When Stanley Gault took over as CEO of Goodyear after a long period of stagnation, he was stunned by repeatedly being told by his management team that "a tire is a tire is a tire is a tire" and that, as a result, tires were a commodity that could not be differentiated. Having spent many years as CEO of Rubbermaid, Mr. Gault knew differently, and he challenged his product development team to reinvent the tire. Within a few months, Goodyear introduced the Aquatread Tire which eliminates "surfing" when driving through water. A few months later, it introduced an improved, dual track, version. As the sales of these two new products have soared, so has the value of Goodyear's stock.

One of our clients, Mooney Chemicals (OMG Group), trades in raw mineral commodities such as cobalt and nickel. Yet Mooney has been able to treat these minerals in such a manner to become the leading provider of carbonoxylates and set itself apart from all its competitors.

Another of our clients trades in clay. That is right—wet mud—the commodity of all commodities! Still, that company has been able to find a wide range of product applications from Kaopectate to kitty litter.

Yet another example is baking soda—one of the world's oldest commodities, until someone at Arm & Hammer saw an application for it in refrigerators to absorb foul odors. This small breakthrough enabled the company to reconsider its conclusion about the commodity status of baking soda. Once the mindset broke, the company started looking for other potential applications and soon found one—toothpaste. Now there are over a dozen brands of toothpaste that contain baking soda—all selling at a premium! What will they think of next? How about Arm & Hammer Anti-Perspirant, which the company just introduced? So much for commodity products.

Then, there is the "mother" of all commodities—water. Yet the French have mastered the marketing of this mundane commodity by branding it under a variety of names such as Vitel, Evian, and Perrier. They have been so successful that their success has attracted the attention of the product innovators/differentiators. And thus the birth of Nordic, which took water and added fruit flavorings such as strawberry, raspberry, and lemon. And then along came Clearly Canadian, which added fruit flavorings and bubbles to give us fruit-flavored, bubbled water. And then another company decided to add tea to the mixture and—voila!—Snapple was born.

The key to not allowing your products to become commodities is to practice a concept we call *market fragmentation*. More will be said about this important concept in a later chapter.

"Only entrepreneurs in small companies can innovate. Large companies stifle risk taking and new product creation."

This is a seductive fallacy that can quickly become an impediment to new product innovation. This is particularly true in the United States because of the large number of companies that have been started by entrepreneurs and the hero worship these founders receive. Henry Ford of Ford Motor Company, Thomas Edison of General Electric, Ray Kroc of McDonald's, Steve Jobs of Apple Computer, Bill Gates of Microsoft, and Fred Smith of Federal Express are but a few such heroes.

Lesser "heroes," however, seldom receive the adulation reserved for entrepreneurs except from other employees of the firms they work for. This is regrettable, because most new product innovations are originated by people who work for someone else.

Some quick examples. All of 3M's 60,000 products are the creation of salaried employees. Post-it Notes came from Spencer Fry, a 3M chemist, and his search for a method to keep track of certain hymns in his prayer book without destroying the words that were printed on each page. A fireproof corrugated box was developed by a group of Digital Equipment employees who were looking for a method to prevent their computers from being destroyed by fire during storage in various warehouses. American Airlines's frequent flier program, a novelty in that industry when first introduced, was the creation of the marketing manager. In 1956, another 3M employee spilled a new chemical on her tennis shoe. Sometime later, she realized that area was not becoming as dirty as the rest of her shoe. The result? A major new product for 3M called Scotchguard Fabric Protector.

These examples, and many more, are the result of *entrepreneurial employees*, not entrepreneurs.

"Innovators are born. It's a trait of personality, and we just don't have any of these people around."

One of the worst impediments to new product creation is the thought that innovation is a trait of personality. In others words, that a few select people are born with that trait while the rest of the masses are not.

As Thomas Edison once observed: "Invention is 10% inspiration and 90% perspiration" (*Edison: Inventing the Century* by Neil Baldwin, Hyperion, 1995). The main reason that many people attribute the skill to personality is that most people who are good at new product creation cannot describe the process, or method, they use. Again, anything that cannot be codified cannot be explained.

Our contention is that the ability of people to innovate is a function of the *management system* in place in an organization rather than a trait of personality. How does one explain the hundreds, or even thousands, of product innovators that 3M has been able to attract to its company? Is it because 3M has an uncanny knack of finding all these people with this trait while its neighbors in St. Paul or its competitors do not? Even 3M isn't that superior in its personnel selection. Obviously, there is something else at work. 3M has, in our opinion, *institutionalized* a process to generate, capture, evaluate, and introduce new products more quickly and more successfully than its competitors.

Another example to prove our hypothesis that innovative behavior is a function of the process and not a trait of personality: China and Hong Kong. Why is it that for 40 years, the Chinese in Hong Kong were so innovative while their brethren on mainland China were not? After all, they share the same genes. What, then, is different? The answer: the system. The economic system in Hong Kong caused innovation to flourish while the communist system in China suppressed innovation. There is even further and more recent proof. Since China has reformed its economic system in the last few years, innovation is starting to be seen on the mainland as well.

It is the *organizational process* used by management that will create an environment conducive to new product innovation. More will be said about the environment and the process that is required to create a culture of new product creation and how it can be fostered in virtually any organization. For now, however, the important point to emphasize is that, although it is true that business owners or so-called entrepreneurs can create new products or markets, it is usually employees in all sizes of companies that provide most new product concepts.

What the innovative organization requires is a method that allows concepts for new products or markets to be gathered and harvested in a systematic manner.

"New product creation is too risky."

Although it is true that new product innovation can be risky, taking extreme risk is not a characteristic of entrepreneurs nor of innovative companies. Donald Trump, one of the premier entrepreneurs of the 1980s, said in his book *The Art of the Deal* (Warner Books, 1989): "I've never gambled in my life. To me, a gambler is someone who plays the slot machines. I prefer to own the slot machines. Less risk."

David Singleton, another entrepreneur, who built a very successful newspaper chain, has also reaffirmed this notion by saying: "To outsiders, our behavior may seem to be risky, but every risk was very carefully calculated" (*USA Today*, November 1990).

The same is true of entrepreneurial organizations. As the former chairman of 3M once said to this author: "I prefer placing 50 small bets than one big bet."

Innovative organizations do take risk, but it is *prudent* risk. They know exactly what risks are there, and they have in place actions to contain such risk, as we will see when we study the process of new product creation and successful introduction in the following chapters.

"We don't have the resources necessary to innovate."

The perception that new product or new market creation requires a lot of resources is another major impediment to innovation. Such is not the case.

As Jeffry Timmons, author of *New Business Opportunities and Planning* (Brick House Publishing, 1990), stated:

> Entrepreneurship is a human, creative act that builds something of value from practically nothing. It is the pursuit of opportunity regardless of the resources, or lack of resources, at hand. It require a vision and the passion and commitment to lead others in the pursuit of that vision. It also requires a willingness to take calculated risks.

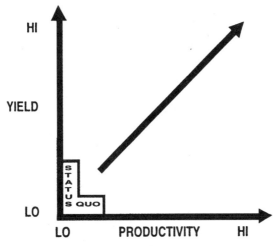

Figure 2-1.

Again, our view is that new product or market opportunities are a function of a firm's ability to manage change together with its constant strive to *redeploy assets and resources from areas of low yield and productivity to areas of higher yield and higher productivity* (see Figure 2-1).

3

The Search for New Product Opportunities

"Where do you find all these new ideas?" we asked several of the most innovative people at 3M, Caterpillar, Johnson & Johnson, and other firms.

"Lightning bolts out of the blue," said one.

"Gut feeling," said another.

"Magic," responded a third person.

In other words, they did not know and could not attribute a source to their innovation. Interestingly, good innovators frequently cannot describe the process they use, and therefore they attribute the skill to all types of irrelevant occurrences. When we observed these people at work, however, we saw them practicing a very deliberate process that they used over and over but could not describe.

Good innovators know where to look for new products or markets. There are ten specific areas of the business that they constantly monitor for changes that can be converted into new opportunities.*

[1]First mentioned in Peter F. Drucker's book: *Innovation and Entrepreneurship*, Harper Business, 1985.

> Unexpected Successes
> Unexpected Failures
> Unexpected External Events
> Process Weaknesses
> Industry/Market Structure Changes
> High-Growth Areas
> Converging Technologies
> Demographic Changes
> Perception Changes
> New Knowledge

As we go through the list and provide examples, we think you'll begin to see what we mean by some organizations not hearing the knock of opportunity and others opening the door but not recognizing it. Not all airlines embraced the frequent-flyer programs at an early stage. In fact, some were dragged kicking and screaming into the programs, despite earlier protestations that they would never provide such give-aways. Not all fountain pen manufacturers were in a position to capitalize on the instrument's new-found cachet. They were not "being in the right place at the right time," and that is not luck. But some organizations are constantly on the lookout for opportunity. Being on such a lookout means having the wherewithal to examine the following sources of potential opportunity with diligence and regularity.

Unexpected Successes

Every organization has events that happen to it that succeed beyond anyone's wildest dreams. A product sells more briskly than anticipated in Montana. Market share goes through the roof in France. Wholesalers, to whom the firm had never expected to sell, start placing large orders. Unfortunately, in too many organizations *unexpected successes* are looked on as temporary aberrations that will quickly return to normal. People who see unexpected successes as temporary aberrations will miss out on a number of future opportunities.

It is also not wise to ignore unexpected successes that competitors may be having. This could be deadly. Such a phenomenon is currently being seen in the fast-food, chicken business. Boston Chicken, which is opening new stores at the rate of one per day—over 300 in 1994 alone—is not yet perceived as a competitor by its rival, Kentucky Fried Chicken. "We're the Queen Mary, and they're some tugboats buzzing around us," says one of their executives. All forgotten in this analogy is the fact that the Queen Mary has been in mothballs for over 25 years. Watch out KFC! Your rival's unexpected success may not be an aberration after all.

Most organizations accept success readily enough, and most recognize it when they experience it. Relatively few companies, however, make that key determination that allows them to build still further on this success. After all, if failures can be exacerbated, why can't successes be exploited? Unexpected successes can happen to both your own organization and those of your competitors. Most people, unfortunately, explain away unexpected successes as temporary aberrations that will soon disappear. Ray Kroc wondered why he was selling so many milkshake machines to a small restaurant run by the McDonald brothers. Only through examining the cause of an unexpected success, as Kroc did, are we able to genuinely exploit change and create innovative new approaches.

Another example occurred in the personal computer field. When personal computers were developed and launched, their manufacturers naturally hoped that they would be successful, but it's safe to say that no one ever dreamed that they would be as successful as they have been. After all, when Steve Jobs and Steve Wozniak were tinkering in their garage building on what turned out to be the first Apple computer, no bank would underwrite their fledgling company, and the two entrepreneurs themselves saw their market as much more limited than it ultimately turned out to be. The personal computer's success was striking enough, but the scope and degree of its success were truly shocking and, consequently, most unexpected.

Jobs was able to exploit that success by very rapidly building one of the major computer firms in the world, Apple Computer. Others, however, were able to capitalize on his success as well. Those who were smart enough to see the market for peripherals and support services also profited nicely. Perhaps the best known example is Bill Gates, who founded and continues to run Microsoft. Gates has recently become the first billionaire in the industry, joining the likes of such legends as Bill Packard and David Hewlett.

The magazine industry was also able to take advantage of the unexpected success of personal computers. Scores of magazines cropped up; some specialized in particular models of computers such as *PC World* and *Mac World*, published for computer users, and other magazines appealed to the programmer and/or "hacker."

Here are some questions that we have found useful to help mine opportunity from unexpected successes. By asking yourself these questions, and by formalizing them as part of your company's work routine, you will tend not to overlook unexpected successes, whether yours or someone else's. Not all the questions may apply, but we find that by asking them in a disciplined fashion, answers to those that do apply tend to reveal the raw material you need to find opportunities for new products or markets.

Process Questions

- What unexpected product success have you had recently?
- In which geographic areas have you had unexpected success recently?
- In which market/industry segments have you experienced unexpected success recently?
- What customer segments have provided unexpected success recently?
- What unexpected successes have your suppliers had recently?
- What unexpected successes have your competitors had recently?
- Which of your technologies has had unexpected success recently?
- What unexpected customer/user groups have bought from you recently?
- What unexpected sources have asked to sample, distribute, or represent your product recently?

Unexpected Failures

Again, every organization has events that cause it to fail miserably. In this case most people tend to spend the rest of their careers defending the failure. Instead, they should be asking, "What caused this failure, and how can we turn it into an opportunity the next time?" A striking example to follow is Ford, which was responsible for the worst new product introduction ever—the Edsel. However, the automaker was smart enough to learn from this failure and, only a few years later, introduced the most successful new car to date—the Mustang.

Unexpected failure may be failure on our own part or failure on our competitor's part. In either case, we're looking for failures that we didn't anticipate. You might say that any failure is one that wasn't anticipated and that everyone plans to be successful in everything they do. To a certain extent, that's correct. But we're talking here of rather dramatic unexpected failures. That is, failures that occurred when great success had been anticipated.

The Edsel's failure was a signal to at least one Ford executive that people were no longer buying cars simply because of the nameplate or because they wanted no more than basic transportation. People were beginning to buy cars because they wanted to make a lifestyle statement. The individual who realized this was named Iacocca. The Mustang was the first, real lifestyle automobile. Ford could have simply licked its wounds and walked away from the Edsel debacle with its tail between its legs. Instead, through Iacocca Ford learned a lesson that it used to create an innovative new car. Unexpected failures occur on a fairly regular basis. We are not trained, however, to look at them in terms of opportunity.

As mergers and acquisitions have accelerated, we've seen many firms—even apparently large, healthy, and vigorous firms—unexpectedly fail to fight off acquisition attempts or succeed in doing so only to severely damage their worth, using "greenmail" or "poison pill" remedies. These unexpected failures of even large organizations to defend themselves against the raiders have presented opportunity to an entire industry of financial analysts, bankers, and attorneys who now specialize in helping organizations fight off such threats. The unexpected inability of organizations to do this for themselves has created opportunity for someone else.

Failures are disliked, so people tend to defend the failure (protect themselves) rather than try to find out what caused it to happen and how to turn it into an opportunity. Here are some questions that will help you learn and benefit from failures:

Process Questions

- What unexpected product failures have you had recently?
- In which geographic areas have you had unexpected failures recently?
- In which market/industry segments have you experienced unexpected failures recently?
- What customer segments have provided unexpected failures recently?
- What unexpected failures have your suppliers had recently?
- What unexpected failures have your competitors had recently?
- Which of your technologies has had unexpected failures recently?
- Which customer/user groups have had unexpected failures recently?
- Which distributors, dealers, and/or agents have had unexpected failures recently?

Unexpected External Events

IBM was merrily following its five-year business plan when Apple introduced the personal computer (PC). To 1BM, this was a totally unexpected event. IBM was, therefore, faced with two options: one was to ignore the event, and the second, which it wisely chose, was to "tweak" its business plan a little and introduce a PC of its own, which became the industry leader. The right question in this instance is, "How can we turn this unexpected external event into a new product or customer?"

One could also make the argument that the birth of Compaq and Dell were the result of IBM's unexpected success in PCs. Unexpected events, like successes and failures, can be internal or external. But here, external events needn't be happening only with your competitors. Such events go on in the world at large.

Unexpected events are ideal sources for true innovative thinkers. For example, with the onset of aircraft hijackings in the 1960s, entire new industries were born. Although many organizations undoubtedly considered hijacking an event totally unrelated to their basic business, some firms that happened to have the technology to produce metal-detecting equipment realized that a tremendous opportunity lay before them. Those that recognized this first were "lightest on their feet," so to speak, and redirected their resources toward this emerging need; these firms entered a multimillion-dollar industry rapidly and gained a predominant market share. This is a classic example of redeploying existing resources and assets for better yield and productivity. Demonstrating that this is not a process that deals only with tangible goods and manufacturing, some firms supplying guard and security services similarly realized that such services would be needed at airports, and they quickly moved into that vacuum. Even though in many cases this was merely a matter of redirecting some training efforts and pursuing contracts from a different source, not all such firms were able to recognize the opportunity and, more important, to rapidly act on it. This example epitomizes what we mean by recognizing opportunity knocking and being able to do something about it.

The unexpected tampering with over-the-counter medical products, such as Tylenol, caused firms intelligent enough and innovative enough to redirect their efforts toward a new need and respond with tamper-resistant packaging. The AIDS epidemic has provided tremendous opportunity for the manufacturers of condoms and latex gloves, the more innovative of which rapidly sought out advertising and distribution methods that never would have been considered earlier. Consequently, we are seeing condom advertising on television for the first time, but only from those manufacturers fast enough, wise enough, and bold enough to pursue this avenue. The following questions will help your firm benefit from unexpected events:

Process Questions
- What unexpected external events have occurred recently?

- What unexpected internal events have occurred recently?
- Have any expected external and internal events combined in an unexpected way recently?

Process Weaknesses

All organizations are composed of various processes, procedures, or systems: a sales order entry system, an accounts payable system, a manufacturing process, a distribution system, a quality audit process, a sales refund procedure, an inventory control system, and so forth, Every process or system in existence has one of three things wrong with it:

1. A bottleneck
2. A weak link
3. A missing link

If we spend a little time identifying and describing the various processes that exist in our organization, and those of our competitors and customers, and then ask, "What bottlenecks, weak links, or missing links are there in these processes and how can we eliminate them?" the query will surely give rise to a number of innovative products that will make these processes more effective.

The process weakness in the Post Office's failure to provide a guaranteed system of reliable next-day delivery created the phenomenal success story of Federal Express. Of course, long before Frederick Smith entered the scene, United Parcel Service was already capitalizing on the Post Office's weakness in distributing parcels and packages. Process weaknesses should be investigated as thoroughly in one's own organization as in that of the competition or a customer. Sometimes merely correcting a process weakness isn't sufficient. True innovation relies upon replacing the weakness with a dramatic improvement, new product, and/or new service. As seen above, process weaknesses can even give birth to new companies.

One of the best examples of a process weakness we know of is that of the Internal Revenue Service. This is a system and an operation that infuriates taxpayers while inefficiently collecting revenues for the government. We've often speculated that if the collection process were turned over to private enterprise, or if a company could compete with the IRS to collect government revenues in return for some portion of the total billings, not only would a private company thrive but the government would collect far greater revenues at much less cost. Perhaps this is an innovation we should hope does not occur.

One of our newspaper clients recently implemented an interesting innovation regarding one of its process weaknesses. The client had found that its system of attracting and collecting billings on classified advertising was highly inefficient. Time deadlines sometimes prevented advertisers from placing last-minute ads. Moreover, telephone lines stayed busy, operators made mistakes, typographical errors occurred for which the newspaper had to "make good," and a host of other gremlins constantly plagued the system. The newspaper took a look at this weakness and decided that, rather than improve the training of the operators, extend phone hours, or double-check copy, it would take the opportunity to enhance classified advertising in general by giving the advertiser a role in the process.The newspaper developed computer software that enabled advertisers to place classified ads directly in the paper by using their own personal computers and a telephone modem.

In this manner, advertisers could place ads right up until the last minute before the deadline, only hours before the printing of the newspaper. There was no longer a need for a "middle man," since the advertiser was communicating directly with the newspaper's computer. An even greater advantage was that any typographical errors were the fault of the advertiser, and therefore the newspaper was no longer responsible for them. Advertisers were highly in favor of the scheme because it gave them total control of their advertising and much more flexibility in their use of the newspaper's space. Consequently, this weak link in the newspaper's process was not improved but totally revamped to provide a greater opportunity and a greater return on existing assets and resources. What began as a process weakness became what one might consider an unexpected success, and the newspaper is exploiting this by looking into software that will enable display advertisers to have similar flexibility, including the ability to design their own layout.

Another company, Roberts' Express, is exploiting an unusual process weakness, one found in the just-in-time inventory system adopted by most companies in the United States and Europe in the last 15 years. Although a very efficient method to manage the flow of components to an assembly plant, the fact is that sometimes the just-in-time system breaks down. An example might be a car assembly plant located in Detroit that receives its engines from Cleveland. When an engine doesn't get there on time, Roberts' Express comes into the picture. The company has 2000 trucks stationed around the country waiting for such a call. While on the phone with the person from the car assembly plant, Roberts (through a satellite system that connects every truck) will locate the truck closest to the supplier's site and promise the customer to pick up and deliver the engine within a 15-minute window at both ends. And, naturally, Roberts will get paid a substantial premium for doing so.

Here are some questions that will help you take advantage of process weaknesses in your firm or in your competition's processes:

Process Questions

- What self-contained processes exist in the organization?

- What process weaknesses exist in our customers' organization?

- What weakness or "missing link" prevents better process performance?

- Why do some processes perform better at some times than at others?

- What bottlenecks do each of these processes have?

- What process weaknesses among our competitors might we be able to improve on?

Industry/Market Structure Changes

When the rules of the game are suddenly changed in an industry, the changes will usually bring on turmoil, meaning threats for some but opportunities for others. When deregulation hit the health care and transportation industries, many firms and executives in these businesses saw only the threats associated with these changes. Some, such as CuraHealth Corporation or Dave Burr of People's Express, saw opportunity. CuraHealth is restructuring traditional approaches to health care by providing mass-produced services that achieve economies of scale and by making profit-oriented assessments of facilities use. Similarly, elder care and catastrophic care are viewed by health care providers as markets to be exploited.

Industry and market structure changes, such as those we see all around us in the telephone, cable television, and health care industries, and in the internationalization of many businesses, are excellent sources of opportunities. These changes have given rise to the likes of MCI, Sprint, and other alternative telephone carriers, as well as to cable television, satellite dishes, and peripheral businesses such as decoders.

Another person who is presently exploiting structural changes in the health care industry is Judy Figge, CEO of In-Home Health, a fast-growing, $110 million company that provides in-home medical services.

The catalyst to create this company was the growing trend of hospitals looking to dismiss their patients more rapidly in an attempt to cut costs. This change in structure of the health care industry has given rise not only to Ms Figge's company but to an entire new industry.

Here are some questions your firm should ask about structural changes:

Process Questions

- What major structural changes are occurring among your customers?

- What major structural changes are occurring in your geographic markets?

- What major structural changes are occurring within your market/industry structure or in the conduct of your business?

- What major structural changes are occurring among your competitors?

- What major structural changes are happening in your customers' businesses?

- What major structural changes are occurring within your regulatory environment?

- What major structural changes are occurring in your supplier relationships?

High-Growth Areas

Companies need growth to perpetuate themselves. Therefore, they need opportunities that could bring more growth than what might be considered normal. To this end, one should search for changes in the present business or related businesses in which growth is occurring faster than growth in gross domestic product (GDP) or population growth. These are the areas that will bring opportunities with exceptional growth.

Why are there as many as 140 PC manufacturers? The reason is simple. The demand for PCs is growing at a rate of 25 to 50 percent per year. In this kind of environment, there is bound to be a lot of turmoil, which creates opportunity.

Areas of high growth are always attention-getters. Such a development occurred immediately after World War II, when the baby boom created new demand for many products and services, demand that was insufficiently anticipated by most organizations.

Many years ago, the retailer R. H. Macy noticed increased sales of small appliances, far beyond expectations. Macy's management had previously decided that small appliances should play only a limited role in the overall offerings of such a department store. In spite of brisk sales, they decided not to increase supply but simply to sell out what supplies they had and to keep their small-appliance sales an established percentage of overall sales. In so doing, of course, they completely missed the opportunity presented by a society in which "modern conveniences" had become equated with success and in which anything that could reduce housework was being eagerly sought out. This void was more than filled by other retailers and other sources of such appliances.

Home videocassette recorders, as everyone suspects, comprise a fairly high-growth area, with penetration beyond most original estimates. What isn't generally known, however, and what has been aggressively pursued by the more innovative retailers, is that the two- and three-VCR home is becoming increasingly common. Just as having two televisions and two telephones is no longer rare and in many cases is the norm so, too, is having two VCRs in any given family. One can be viewed while another is time-shifting programs, or one can be used by the parents and another by the kids. In any case, here's a high-growth area on top of a high-growth area, if you will. This is the kind of nuance that true innovators look for in their pursuit of opportunity.

You and your colleagues should be constantly asking, "What parts of our business are growing faster than economic or population growth?" Yet we find that high growth is one of the most overlooked of the 10 areas of opportunity search. One reason is that people are more attuned to looking for poor growth than to looking for high growth.

Here are some questions your firm should be asking about economic or population growth:

Process Questions

- What parts of the business are growing faster than economic or population growth?

- What other businesses are growing faster than economic or population growth?

- What potentially high-growth businesses related to yours are dominated by only one or two companies?

- What parts of your competitors' businesses are growing faster than economic or population growth?

- What parts of your customers' or suppliers' businesses are growing faster than economic or population growth?

Converging Technologies

When two or more technologies start to merge, that convergence is
bound to produce turmoil and, as a result, opportunity. The convergence of telecommunication and computer technologies that we have
been witnessing for the last 15 years created turmoil which was perceived initially by AT&T as a major threat but was perceived as a
major opportunity by NEC, Northern Telecom, MCI, and Rolm. Rather
than attempt to defend itself against these opportunities, as AT&T did
(to its regret), these organizations sought to encourage this change
with products and services that exploited it.

Here we are speaking about two or more technologies that perhaps
singly do not represent opportunity but that, when taken together, represent substantial opportunity for those willing to look for it. For
example, the marriage of the computer to the videodisk has created an
interactive learning combination that several training firms have been
in the forefront of perfecting. This combination allows the learner to
see a vignette presented on a television monitor and to respond to it
on a keyboard. Various branching operations allow the learner to view
different vignettes depicting the outcomes that the learner has chosen.

A variation of this can be seen in automobile showrooms, where the
customer may ask the salesperson a question such as, "What does the
car look like in red?" If the salesperson doesn't have a red car available, there's a major problem. Is the salesperson supposed to say to
this customer: "Go visit our competitor who has a red one, and if you
like it, come back here and purchase it from us"? The salesperson
knows that if the customer leaves to find a red car, he or she probably
won't be back. And the various color swatches and chips of paint that
were provided can't provide a very good idea, even for the most conceptual and visual among us.

Now, however, the customer can sit down at a computer/videodisk
machine and, in effect, design a car. If the customer wants to see a
Thunderbird in fire-engine red, one is shown on the screen (under the
best possible lighting and environmental conditions, of course). If the
customer wants to see the sports package, or the leather upholstery, or
how a tire is changed, all this can be viewed while sitting in one place
under the watchful eye and with the attentive help of the salesperson.

In the insurance industry, the convergence of personal computers
and telecommunication networks is revolutionizing the way you get a
cracked windshield replaced. In the past, you would go to an auto
glass repair shop, obtain a quote, submit it to your insurance company
for approval, return to the auto glass shop for the replacement, then
submit your claim to the insurance company and then the insurer
would remit a check to you individually. With the advent of PCs and

networks, the system works very differently. Most insurers have now "licensed" certain auto glass repair shops into a nationwide network. If you were to crack your windshield today, you would be referred to the closest shop in the insurer's network, have the windshield replaced immediately at a prearranged price between the insurer and the repair shop, and then the insurer would send the shop a monthly check for all the replacements done during that month—a system more user friendly for the customer and more cost effective for the insurer.

In fact, rather than wait for the convergence to occur, it is much better to cause it to happen. Such is the case in a number of alliances that have recently been formed. For example, AT&T and Novell are planning to link business telephone and PC networks into a system to ease the retrieval of messages. Microsoft and Tele-Communications are getting together to deliver video-on-demand through cable lines and PCs, using Microsoft software. CNN and Intel are merging broadcasting technology with personal computers to bring business information directly into offices. In a three-way convergence, Zenith, Philips, and Compression Labs are linking to develop television set-top boxes for interactive cable TV programs.

These questions can help your firm look for technology-based opportunities:

Process Questions

- What technologies in your business are converging or merging?

- Which of your technologies is now being joined to outside technologies?

- Which of your technologies can be more effective if deliberately converged?

- What would be the ideal convergence of technologies in your business?

Demographic Changes

The demographics of an organization's customers are not static. They change with time. As a result, if a company attempts to anticipate the demographic changes that will occur in its customer base in the future, it's bound to find opportunity. For example, if one looks at the current phenomenon of the aging of the United States, one should be able to see nothing but opportunities.

Four categories of demographic changes need to be monitored in a firm's end customers:

1. Income
2. Age
3. Education
4. Mix

The right question is, "What demographic changes are happening or will happen in our end customers in these four areas, and how can we convert these into new product or market opportunities?"

Demographic change is interesting because sometimes it's subtle, and sometimes it is rather rapid. Demographics, of course, can involve such things as the age or education of your users, their income, where they are living, the mix of users, and so on. We mentioned gentrification earlier. We have found that many managers are still laboring under the illusion that the youth market, the so-called Yuppie market, is the preeminent buying market in the economy. This is not true. Rather, the "gray market" is expanding more rapidly and possesses the greatest potential buying power. This is why we see innovative companies providing distinct products and services to this user group. Things like leisure communities for people over a certain age have long been with us, but now we are seeing leisure resorts, travel agencies catering only to people over 50 years of age, and advertising aimed specifically at this age group.

However, in the next 10 years, the teen market (12–16 years) will be the second fastest growing with a population that will increase from 20 to 30 million. This growth will present a multitude of new product opportunities. The magazine business has already detected the opportunity, and two new publications aimed at this market were introduced this month alone.

Another significant demographic change happening in the United States is the increasing importance of the "ethnic" market. The United States is no longer a WASP domain but is fast becoming an ethnic mosaic which will bring numerous product creation opportunities as well.

How dramatic is demographic change? Here's a quick example from the United States: A man who is married to his first wife, who is the sole breadwinner in his family, and who has two children and a house in the suburbs, now represents less than 4 percent of the population. That's right, less than 4 percent. Not too many years ago, such a man would have seemed relatively "average." Today, however, with nearly 50 percent of marriages ending in divorce, almost 60 percent of women working outside the home, and more people employed by McDonald's than by U.S. Steel, demographic change can sneak up on us. Sneaky or not, however, it presents tremendous opportunity.

Demographic changes have long been used by direct-mail advertisers, political analysts, and aggressive marketers. Such changes, however, can represent opportunity for anyone, irrespective of his or her business and its products or services.

Sometime in the years ahead, there will be an unprecedented infusion of money into the economy. Where will it come from? It will come from the IRA funds that will have built up over a 10- or 20-year or even longer period and will have provided a retired and educated population with a greater affluence than has ever been known before. The tax legislation that provided for these IRAs will be producing a dramatic monetary change in the population, decades after its enactment. In the next few years, the first large amounts of IRA money will start to be withdrawn and will be followed by larger and larger withdrawals. The opportunities will abound for people who are capable of helping IRA recipients to invest, spend, safeguard, and provide for the ultimate redistribution of those funds.

A side consequence of these plans is that there will also be an enormous transfer of wealth from one generation to another. It is projected that the baby boomers of this generation will be inheriting $10.4 trillion from 1990 to 2040—for a mean inheritance of $90,000 per person. What will these inheritors do with all their new wealth? They probably will be looking around to spend it with companies that have been astute enough to detect this trend and create new products and services tailored to this emerging need.

Here are some questions about demographics your firm can be asking:

Process Questions

- How is the age distribution of your customers and users changing?
- How will the educational level of your customers and users change in the next few years?
- How will the income distribution of your customers and users change in the next few years?
- How will the geographic distribution of your customers and users change in the years ahead?
- How might the buying habits of your customers and users change in the years ahead?
- What are the customer demographics that might change over the years ahead?
- How will the mix of your users and customers change in the next few years?

Perception Changes

How your customers perceive your products changes with time. If you can anticipate the changes of perception that your customers have or will have vis-à-vis your products, you are bound to find opportunity. For example, the automobile was once perceived strictly as a mode of transport. In the 1960s, however, Ford's Lee Iacocca detected that some people perceived the automobile to be a reflection of their lifestyles, and came out with the Mustang—the first lifestyle car.

The right question to ask is, "What changes are happening in how our customers perceive our products, and how can we convert these changes into new opportunities?"

This search area is unique in that it is the only one that can be consciously manipulated. After all, that's what advertising is all about, attempting to achieve changes in perception. Note that changes in perception are not changes in the facts themselves but rather changes in how people choose to interpret the facts.

Such changes in perception are common and dramatic. For example, people have been driving while drinking since the automobile was invented nearly a century ago. But it's only within the last few years that the true danger of driving while under the influence of alcohol has been underscored and brought to the U.S. public's attention, with the resulting stigma on such activity. Similarly, perceptions of personal fitness, the hazards of smoking, the importance of preventing certain diseases, and other health matters have changed radically.

In working with a *Fortune* 500 client, we noted one division experiencing increasing difficulty in selling microfilm for archival use. Ten years ago, microfilm was perceived as high-tech. Today, electronics is perceived as high-tech and microfilm as low-tech. Although microfilm is still the best available alternative (the product and its usefulness have not changed), in most cases the customer's perception of the product has changed substantially.

How have entrepreneurs capitalized on perception change? Well, we've seen the decline of the "happy hour" and the singles bar and the corresponding rise of the health club. It seems as though the place to meet young, eligible, single people these days is no longer in the singles bar but in the health club. Tobacco companies have rushed to diversify their businesses in response to the public's growing concern over the perils of tobacco smoking. Brewers and distillers have moved toward lighter alcoholic beverages, low-calorie beverages, and nonalcoholic beverages. From the same supplier, you can now buy sodas with any combination of no-caffeine, no-sugar, and no-carbohydrates.

Although some changes in perception come belatedly, such as recognizing the risks of tobacco, and some merely achieve greater prominence, such as the danger of driving while drinking, others are deliberately created. For example, perfume advertisements create the perception that its use will create erotic interludes. Such advertising is not limited to the private sector. The armed forces have been able to completely change the public perception of the military in the post-Vietnam era. The Marines now advertise for "a few good men." The Army advertises its ability to train people for high-paying professional careers after their service career is over. The Army's current advertising slogan is, "Be all that you can be."

Too often, companies waste money trying to improve the product, or improve its distribution, or better train the sales force when in fact what's needed is a change in the public's perception of the product. No matter what Schaeffer or Waterman appears to be able to do, neither has been able to create the same perception of quality as has Cross pens. Rolex has dominated the public's perception as the best watch on the market, as has Mercedes as the high-class automobile. These last two examples clearly point out one benefit of achieving a changed perception: You can then charge for the perception. Let's face it, no Mercedes is worth the amount of money that it costs to purchase one. The engineering may be superb, and the styling may be excellent, but a good portion of the purchase price represents the perceived prestige that rolls along with it. Years ago, some forgotten innovator determined that the public will pay for perception, and it's a lesson that Mercedes et al. have not forgotten.

Sometimes, changes in perception can bring major setbacks if you are not careful. Such is the case with the Lacoste tennis shirts. Introduced some 50 years ago by French tennis hero Rene Lacoste, it was positioned as an upper-class shirt with a certain cachet. Appropriately, it was made of 100 percent cotton and premium priced. When General Mills purchased the brand in the early eighties, it decided to license the name to a wide variety of unrelated products covering the entire range of price points with total disregard for the name's "upper crust" perception by its traditional customers. When these customers noticed the downgrading of the name to the point where it was appearing on anything from low-priced tennis shoes to T-shirts, they left the brand in droves. Lacoste's revenues of tennis shirts dropped from $500 million to less than $50 million in three years. A major shift in how Lacoste customers perceived the brand name had occurred and caused the decline.

Black & Decker is another company that, to its favor, caused an important change in perception to occur. The company, as we all know, is famous for its small building tools. These have traditionally been very popular with the do-it-yourselfer but have never been well received by the professional tradesperson. The tradesperson saw it as "beneath his (or her) dignity" to use a tool that the less sophisticated, home do-it-yourselfer used. As result, Black & Decker's sales to the tradesperson have never gone anywhere. Until the company decided to dust off an old brand name—DeWalt—it had used many years before. It then set our to repackage its tools with a new logo and color and at a higher price. But the product is exactly the same. It also started calling on tradespeople on job sites and espousing the benefits of the DeWalt tools. The change in perception was engineered extremely well, and the results have been better than expected. Today the company has grown its DeWalt division to revenues of $300 million while maintaining its dominant position in the do-it-yourself market.

So perception is very important in innovation. You should examine your current products and services, both for their vulnerability to perception change and for your ability to change perception of them. Perception change is fickle. It can happen on the spur of the moment, almost before you realize what's taken place. Only by diligently and consistently scanning the environment and surveying your own operation as well as those of your competitors will you be able to stay ahead and therefore profit from the opportunity of perception change.

These questions will help your firm focus on perception changes:

Process Questions

- What changes are occurring in how your products and services are *perceived?*

- What changes are occurring in the *values* of your customers?

- What changes are occurring in the *lifestyle, image,* and *status* of your customers?

- How will changes in perception *affect* your customers and suppliers?

- For what *new purposes* have customers purchased your products and services recently?

- What *intangible* reasons are customers developing to support your products and services?

- What societal, peer, and normative *pressures* will affect your products and services in the future?

These questions could also be asked of your customer's customer if you are a business-to-business firm.

New Knowledge

New knowledge means inventions, discoveries, patents, and the like. Obviously discoveries, or new knowledge, will always lead to opportunities in the form of new products or markets. However, inventions can take a long time to commercialize into profitable products. Fiber optics and lasers were invented in 1955 and are only now beginning to be converted into successful products. History has shown that inventions can take as long as 25 years to become commercially viable. Therefore, it is wise to seek innovations in some of the other nine areas first. New knowledge probably represents the basis for most new patents granted, year in and year out. But very few of those patents ever result in a viable, marketable product.

New knowledge has some intrinsic barriers. For one thing, new knowledge, or pure invention, often takes large amounts of research and experimentation, as well as a long time to develop. Second, the window of opportunity in new knowledge is often severely limited. For example, new knowledge is usually applicable for only a brief time. Or if it is applicable over a long period, new knowledge is difficult to protect from the inroads of competitors, patents, and copyrights. So new knowledge is perhaps the most difficult of all the areas of opportunity search, yet it nonetheless produces significant opportunity. Merck & Company is an example of one of the more innovative firms. Over the years, Merck's innovation has come almost exclusively from its research and development efforts, from the new knowledge it's been able to generate through its laboratories and scientists. New knowledge can be an excellent source of opportunity if it's explored carefully and systematically.

The laser is an excellent example of new knowledge. It has provided industrial, military, communications, and health care uses. Note the diversity of application that this one bit of new knowledge has created. Don't assume that new knowledge has to be specifically related to your products and services. The true innovator finds distinct and discrete applications of new knowledge that can benefit his or her particular business. Superconductors are the latest new knowledge breakthrough, with major implications for industries ranging from communications to transportation.

Here are some questions about new knowledge your firm can ask:

Process Questions

- What new knowledge has recently become known about your business?

- What combinations of knowledge have created new insights into your business?

- What new sources of information about your business have recently been tapped?

- What new patents or discoveries have been announced relating to your business?

Observations Regarding the Search Step

During our work with client organizations, we have made several critical observations regarding how these companies go about finding new product or market opportunities. First, all the organizations with which we have worked to date were bombarded by changes from all 10 areas simultaneously.

Lesson number one in corporate life is that no organization is immune to change. The only constant is change, and any organization that tries to hide or protect itself from change through regulation, legislation, or artificial barriers is doomed to complacency and eventual failure. As much as some people may resent it, innovation is creative destruction of the status quo, something that the best companies are constantly looking to disrupt.

Second, the best companies do not wait for these changes to occur before responding. In fact, wherever applicable, these companies will be the ones to initiate changes.

Third, there is a direct relationship between the probability of finding opportunity and its source on the list of ten search areas. The further down the list you must go to find opportunity, the less likely you will be to succeed. The reason is simple. The further it is down the list, the more difficult the change will be to detect and to convert into a successful opportunity. Nonetheless, this is where we found many organizations looking, at the expense of passing by a host of potential opportunities from the top of the list which are easier to detect and exploit.

Fourth, most organizations that were being bombarded by these 10 types of changes had the tendency to see only the threats associated with them, overlooking the opportunities. It was usually people outside the organization who saw the opportunities. A winning organization deals with the threats but demands that the organization and its people translate these changes into opportunities as well. As Peter Drucker wrote in *Innovation and Entrepreneurship* (Harper Business, 1985), "Resources, to produce results, must be allocated to opportunities rather than to problems."

Last, innovative companies do not count on home runs or the big bang approach to innovation. If they do come across big bang ideas, all the better. In the meantime, however, innovative companies believe in and practice continuous, marginal, incremental innovation in every aspect of the business and on the part of everyone in the organization.

The 10 areas of changes discussed above are the primary sources of product innovation, the areas from which product opportunities can best be derived. But what of the bright idea, the miracle cure, the conceptual breakthrough? They have all played their part, to be sure, and patents are issued every day on inventions based on them, some of which are successfully implemented in the marketplace. Yet they aren't the source that organizations generally rely on, nor are they the sources that lend themselves to a process. They are not repeatable on demand, cannot be taught and learned, and are seldom immediately applicable. Great ideas shouldn't be ignored when encountered, but neither should they be relied upon to assist in innovation on a daily basis. It's like finding a $10 bill in the street. You're glad it was there, and you certainly can use it, but you wouldn't leave your house hoping to find one to pay for the groceries that day.

Categories of New Opportunities

Many organizations, even ones who do innovate well, have difficulty categorizing the "types" of new products they create. When is a new product new and not just an extension? From our work with clients over the years, we have come to identify the following categories of product innovation.

The first is a *new-to-the-market product.* These are products that have never been seen before. An example is 3M's introduction of Post-it Notes or Sony's introduction of the Walkman. New-to-the-market products usually create entire new *markets.*

A second category is *new-to-us.* These are product categories that already exist but in which our company has no entry. They are usually introduced by a competitor. An example is General Mill's attempts to clone Kellogg's Corn Flakes or Panasonic's clone of Sony's Walkman. Although usually clones, these are nonetheless sources of new product revenue for the cloning company.

The third category is *product extension,* and this category has two subsets. On the one hand are product extensions that represent *marginal* or *incremental* improvements to an existing product. An example is 3M's extension of its original 1-in by 1-in Post-it Note into a wide

Figure 3-1. Airbus plans an 800-passenger airplane.

range of different sizes. The other product extension is a little more dramatic. This can be called a *quantum leap* improvement. An example, again, is 3M's introduction of Post-it Notes in a pop-up box such as the manner in which Kleenex tissues are offered. This type of product extension is a little more difficult to conceive and achieve and may give the company access to new customers or markets.

Another good example is Airbus's recent announcement that it will construct an 800-passenger airplane (see Figure 3-1). Although an extension of a current product, it will be a gargantuan task to create an airplane 2.5 times larger than the largest, 350-seat model.

The last category is *new customers and/or markets*. These are products that, relatively unchanged, can lead to new classes of customers, new market segments, or new geographic markets. Although these are not new product innovations in the real sense of the term, they do, nonetheless, represent new sources of revenue for the company and may require some degree of innovative thinking before they can be capitalized upon.

Articulating New Product Concepts

After using the process questions in this chapter, it is not unusual to generate a list of 50 to 60 new concepts for products, customers, or markets. It is imperative, at this stage, that these new concepts be articulated in words specific and succinct enough that those taking them through the remainder of the process described in this book can "get their arms around them." In other words, the concepts need to be described in terms clear enough that one can put physical boundaries around them in order to be able to evaluate their potential in the next step of this process. In fact, if one can "draw a picture" of the new concept, even better.

Figure 3-2. A new product idea—cellular telephone, diary, and paging device in one instrument with a modem to transmit messages.

The following is an example. While working with a manufacturer of cellular telephones in the United Kingdom, a group in the work session started discussing the "unexpected success" of the File-o-Fax diary system offered in all the airports in the country. Out of this source of innovation, they conceived a new product they would call a Filo-Fone. It would consist of a combination cellular telephone, diary, and paging device—all with a modem to transmit messages. In order to explain the concept to their colleagues, they drew a picture of it (see Figure 3-2).

The Opportunity Generation Machine

The *search step* allows you to explore every nook and cranny of the business and its environment looking for potential new product or new market opportunities. By systematically examining these areas as part of your daily business routine, we can almost guarantee that

CHANGE	OPPORTUNITY	POTENTIAL NEW PRODUCT CONCEPT
▪ Unexpected Succsses		
▪ Unexpected Failures		
▪ Unexpected External Events		
▪ Process Weaknesses		
▪ Industry/Market Structure Changes		
▪ High-Growth Areas		
▪ Converging Technologies		
▪ Demographic Changes		
▪ Perception Changes		
▪ New Knowlege		

Figure 3-3. The search step—identifying the change, looking for the opportunity, and establishing new product concepts.

your organization will benefit dramatically. When looking at each of the search areas, it's important to first identify the particular event—unexpected success, demographic change, change in perception—that might be relevant. This is the ore that you've found in the ground. The next step is to look for opportunities in those events, that is, to extract the ore from the ground. The final part of the search step is to establish specific and detailed product concepts that can flow from this opportunity (see Figure 3-3). This is the cleaning and polishing of the ore that we hope you've discovered to be gold. The important effort is to identify opportunities and not to worry about their source. It is not important whether an opportunity came from unexpected success, a competitor's process weakness, or a high-growth area. Just identify it. The process does not give points for neatness. In other words, it doesn't matter which area generates the opportunity, so long as it is generated. That's why we have posed so many different process questions. The goal is to identify the opportunity, no matter what its source.

The New Opportunity Hopper

After this first step in the process, you now have a hopper full of new product or market concepts (Figure 3-4). To keep the hopper full, it

Figure 3-4. The new opportunity hopper.

now becomes important to repeat the search step at regular intervals, since the only constant is change. It is wise to keep the hopper full so that, when required, a company can simply reach into its hopper for another new product concept. In other words, by periodically repeating the search step, the well never goes dry. Of course, the next step is to visit the assayer's office to determine how much the gold is worth and to make sure that it's not simply fool's gold. We call that the *opportunity assessment step*, the second step in the product innovation process.

4
New Product Opportunity Assessment

As a result of the search step, we now face a multitude of opportunities for new products, services, customers, or markets. As any good innovator knows, not all opportunities are worth pursuing. The second step of product innovation is to assess all the opportunities against certain criteria in order to rank them in terms of their potential to the organization.

The problem is not that opportunity knocks but once, but that it is knocking every day in the multitude of changes facing organizations. We have found—initially to our own surprise, and always to the surprise of clients—that organizations have a surplus of opportunities. Once they are recognized, the real challenge of management is to differentiate among them and to select those that promise the greatest potential benefit within the company's basic business plan.

Just as in problem solving and decision making (where difficulty usually arises not from an absence of information but from too much information, information which is often contradictory), difficulties in product innovation arise from having too many opportunities to deal with and too many factors to consider. Therefore, there is all the more need for some filtering or winnowing process that will allow the organization to make intelligent choices about the best opportunities to pursue.

As in any good idea-generating process, the search step should produce new ideas without negative comment. Its intent is to provide a clear thinking and free thinking base from which to generate new ideas. The assessment step provides the means to evaluate these ideas and to critically analyze them for their ability to meet parameters as we have defined them: shifting existing assets and resources from areas of low productivity and yield to areas of high productivity and yield. Consequently, you are also able to evaluate existing uses of those assets and resources in this step.

Assessment begins the analysis of how well the new opportunity fits your business and your culture and helps to analyze risk, so that pet projects aren't insulated from real consequences. Finally, the assessment step begins the identification of critical factors that will determine the ultimate success of the concept arising from the opportunity, so that when and if you reach the implementation stage you are armed with a plan to ensure success. Too many great opportunities die on the drawing board or are mortally wounded when the conceptualizer and the implementer are different people or different groups. New product creation has to result in successful implementation, and the assessment step is the first stop along that route.

How are new product or market concepts and alternatives currently decided upon in your organization? Often the loudest voice or highest position will determine which approaches receive proper resources. Sometimes the squeaky wheel gets the resources. At other times, simply the safest—or at least, what is *perceived* as the safest—course of action is chosen. Still other times, what's been done in the past determines future actions—not terribly daring decision making, but at least it's terribly safe. The assessment step provides an objective template not only for judging new concepts against each other but also for judging new concepts against existing uses of assets and resources. In this way, the true value of redeploying those assets and resources to achieve higher productivity and yield can be visibly and tangibly evaluated.

The Four Assessment Areas

We have isolated four key areas that we believe encompass the essential criteria for assessing new product concepts: cost, benefit, strategic fit, and difficulty of implementation. These four areas have subsets and can be further divided, tailored, and modified to best represent your organization and its culture. We have learned, however, that, as in most management practices, the ideal process is not necessarily the most complicated or complex one. Rather, the ideal process can be used quickly by an individual and/or efficiently and harmoniously by a group, no matter how disparate its members. Consequently, although we've found that many groups tend to modify or detail the criteria underlying each major area, we have not found any group or organization that feels the need to change the four basic areas.

Cost-Benefit Relationship

The first two criteria are obvious enough—*cost* and *benefit*. Each opportunity needs to be assessed in terms of its relative cost versus relative benefit. In fact, a visual grid (the assessment grid in Figure 4-1) can be used to show where each opportunity falls.

Anyone engaged in product creation and introduction should want to know fairly concisely and rapidly: What will be the cost of implementing this opportunity? And what will be the benefit of implementing this opportunity? Some of the generic questions usually asked include:

- What is the cost of this new product or market opportunity?
- What is the benefit of this new product or market opportunity?

The following is a checklist of considerations to assess that contribute either to the potential cost or potential benefit of an opportunity. An evaluation of each will allow you to create a framework within which the cost-benefit relationship can be clarified and scrutinized.

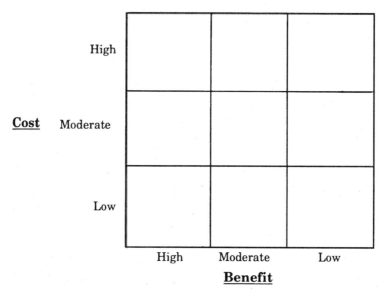

Figure 4-1. Cost-benefit assessment grid. (*Copyright by Decision Processes International. All rights reserved.*)

Checklist

Cost	Benefit
Cost	*Benefit*
People	Market share
Materials	Return/profit
Equipment	Prestige/image
Research	Service/satisfaction
Marketing	Earnings/dividends
Legal	Fallout/residuals
Promotion	Safety/security
Time	Quality
Pilot	Morale/motivation
Contingency	Growth/size

Strategic Fit/Difficulty of Implementation Relationship

The next two assessment criteria are less obvious—*strategic fit and difficulty of implementation*. These two criteria are probably more important than the cost-benefit ratio, but unfortunately they are almost always overlooked.

Strategic Fit.   How well does this new product or market opportunity fit the strategy of the business? This is a key question that is often not asked but should be. Experience has shown that organizations that try to innovate *outside the strategic framework* of the business usually do not succeed.

By strategic fit, we mean the degree to which an opportunity fits a company's direction. The opportunity need not fit exactly at first, provided that it promises to fit well in the near future. So the issue concerns not just today's strategy but also the direction that the company is pursuing.

When an opportunity is pursued irrespective of strategic thrust, the results are usually disappointing or even damaging. Several years ago, Exxon decided to enter the office information business and began an operation known as QXT. Despite the infusion of massive amounts of money and the work of some highly talented people, QXT was a disaster, and Exxon eventually dissolved it. The office products market simply was not a part of Exxon's direction and strategy as a company. That is, it could not be *made* a part of the nature and direction—the fabric—of Exxon's business. Consequently, it was doomed to failure from the start. A senior executive of Exxon recently told us that Exxon executives did not understand the office equipment business as well as they did the "trivia of the oil business," and thus they could not manage or even judge the opportunities of the former. There was *no* strategic *fit*.

Similarly, People Express seemed to be making good headway toward its own goals when it was forced out of the sky by its acquisition of Frontier Airlines, a traditional carrier that did not fit very well with the vision and direction established by Donald Burr for People's Express.

New product or new market creation is not a question of unbridled enthusiasm spinning off into every direction of the compass at once. It is a question of organized, purposeful, and *focused* attempts to improve the organization's products, services, markets, and operations in general. The end result of innovation has to be an enhanced ability to meet and exceed the organization's *business goals*. Consequently, innovation must be undertaken within the purview of corporate strategy and its *future strategic profile*.

Determining the Future Strategic Profile of the Organization.
How do we go about describing the future profile or an organization? The answer is simple. The "look" or profile of an organization is determined by the nature of its *products, customers, market segments,* and *geographic markets*. Therefore, if management wants to guide the direction of the organization and influence its eventual look, it must determine, in advance, which products, customers, market segments, and geographic markets it *will pursue,* as well as which products, customers, market segments, and geographic markets it *will not pursue* (see Figure 4-2).

Strategically, it is more important to know to what the strategy does not lend itself than it is to know to what it does. Management performs two critical tasks that set the direction of the organization and influence its eventual look. First, management allocates resources. Allocating resources strategically means giving more resources to the areas of the future strategic profile that the company wants to emphasize. In other words, activities that will bring in products, customers, market segments, and geographic markets that resemble items on the left side of our profile will get preferential treatment. Activities that will bring items that resemble those on the right side of our profile will not get resources.

The second most important strategic task of management is to identify which opportunities the organization should *and should not* be pursuing. The future strategic profile is again the final filter for these. Opportunities that will bring the firm items that resemble the ones on the left side will receive preferential treatment over those that do not. With a profile articulated in this manner and imbedded in the heads of

Figure 4-2. (*Copyright by Decision Processes International. All rights reserved.*)

all the key people in the organization, we can now start to manage strategically. This profile becomes the ultimate test bed for all decisions made in the organization.

The next question that comes to mind is, how do we go about determining the line of demarcation between the items that will receive more emphasis and those that will receive less emphasis in the future? The answer to this question gives rise to the most important concept of strategic thinking.

The Concept of Driving Force. The true test to determine whether an organization has a strategy is to watch management when it is faced with the decision of whether to pursue a certain opportunity. During such discussions we noted that although management used a hierarchy of different filters, the ultimate filter was always whether there was a fit between the products, customers, and markets that the opportunity brought and *one* key component of the business. In other words, one part of the business seemed to be strategically more important to managers than all others. If they found a good fit there, they would more than likely pursue that opportunity; if they did not find a good fit, they would not. However, the one element of the business that seemed to be the final filter varied from one company to another. In each company, then, there seemed to be something that was at the root of that company's existence and was pushing, propelling, or *driving* it forward. One component of the business seemed to dominate management thinking. This was its strategic heartbeat and the *driving force** of the business.

When exploring this concept further, we found that there are basically 10 components to any business. These are:

1. Product/service concept

2. Market type/category

3. User/customer class

4. Production capacity/capability

5. Technology/know-how

6. Sales/marketing method

7. Distribution method

8. Natural resources

9. Size/growth

10. Return/profit

The ability of management to clearly understand what strategic area of the business is driving the business and serves as its heartbeat is fundamental to that management team's ability to make intelligent choices about future products, customers, market segments, and geographic markets. Failure to understand this key concept is what leads to strategic ineffectiveness.

Product Concept–Driven Company. A product concept–driven company is locked into a singular product *concept* of some kind whose function and look do not change much over time. Future products are adaptations, modifications, or extensions of the current product. In other words, future product offerings emanating from such a company are derivatives of the existing product, and the existing product is a "genetic" linear extrapolation of its original product.

The automobile industry, in general, is a good example. The look and function of the automobile has not changed for a hundred years and probably will not change for the next hundred. GM, Ford, Toyota, and

---

*From Michel Robert, *Strategy Pure and Simple: How Winning CEOs Outthink Their Competition,* McGraw-Hill, Inc., New York, 1993.

Chrysler are all pursuing a product-driven strategy. Other companies following such a concept are Boeing, with its concept of a "flying machine"; insurance companies, with "risk reduction" as a concept; and heavy-equipment manufacturers, who keep making derivatives of their existing machines. IBM is locked into the concept of "computing machines," and, as such, computers of various sizes are what it produces.

Market Category–Driven Company. This company is very different from the product-driven firm. A market-driven company is one that has deliberately anchored its business to a describable category of market. That market, then, is the only one it serves. The firm's strategy is to continuously scrutinize that market in an attempt to identify related needs. Once these needs are found, then appropriate products, which may otherwise be unrelated to each other, are made.

One example is American Hospital Supply. In its very name, this company has identified the market to which its business is anchored—the hospital. The strategy of the company is to respond to a variety of needs coming from that market. As a result, the product scope of such a firm ranges from bedpans to sutures and from gauze pads to electronic imaging systems. These products are unrelated to each other—not genetic derivatives. The only common thread is that they are all used in a hospital.

User Class–Driven Company. This company's strategy is similar to a market category–driven firm except that this company has anchored its business to a discrete *class* of end users. Johnson & Johnson's strategy of making products for "doctors, nurses, patients, and mothers" is a good example.

Production Capacity/Capability–Driven Company. A capacity-driven strategy is usually pursued by a company that has a substantial investment in its production facility, and the thrust is to keep that facility operating at maximum capacity. The drive is to look for opportunities that can utilize whatever the production capacity can handle. Paper companies, because of enormous capital tied up in their mills, are examples of organizations that usually pursue a capacity-driven strategy. These companies will get into newsprint, fine paper, toilet tissue, disposable diapers, paper towels, and other products in order to optimize their production capacity. A production capability–driven company has built some unique capabilities into its production process and pursues only opportunities that can utilize these unique capabilities. Specialized printers are good examples.

Technology/Know-How–Driven Company. This company has the ability to invent or acquire hard or soft technology or know-how. Then it goes out looking for applications of that technology or know-how. Over time such a company gets involved in a broad array of products, all of which stem from the particular technology, and serves a broad array of customers and market segments. Du Pont and 3M are good examples of such companies.

Sales/Marketing Method–Driven Company. This company has a unique way of attracting orders from its customers. Such a company will only offer products and pursue customers that can be brought together through that selling method. Door-to-door companies such as Mary Kay, Tupperware, and Amway are good examples. Catalogue companies are another. Any product that can be advertised in the catalogue will be considered.

Distribution Method–Driven Company. This company pursues a strategy that is the opposite of that of a sales/marketing method–driven firm. This company has in place a unique distribution system to get products to the customers. All products or services offered must utilize that distribution method, or they will not be offered. Telephone operating companies, with their vast networks, are good examples of such companies. Department stores are another. Sears Roebuck, with its 600 stores across the United States, will push through any product to any customers that they can match with it, from furniture to financial services.

Natural Resources–Driven Company. When pursuit of, or access to, natural resources becomes the strategic drive of an organization, such a company can be perceived as pursuing a resources-driven strategy. Energy companies are examples of such organizations. Exxon, Newmont Mining, and Consolidated Goldfields are such companies.

Size/Growth–Driven Company. A company whose only criterion for getting in or out of business is an appetite for size and growth is motivated by this driving force. Conglomerates that pursue growth for the sake of growth, as W. R. Grace did for many years, are good examples.

Return/Profit–Driven Company. When profit becomes the only criteria for getting in or out of businesses, then such a company is allowing this driving force to dominate its strategy. For such a company, any purchase, and virtually any opportunity, is sound so long as that opportunity generates the appropriate degree of profit. At one time, for example, the Transamerica Company owned a chartered airline, a relocation service, Occidental Insurance, Budget Rent-a-Car, and the United Artists motion picture company, among other organizations. Transamerica's strategy was focused on profit: As long as a certain profit was generated, the subsidiary fit into the overall structure. If the profit couldn't be generated, then the subsidiary no longer fit. We've seen the same hold true for conglomerates such as Gulf & Western and the "old" ITT under Harold Geneen.

At this point, we would like to pose these questions:

- Which driving force mentioned above is currently acting as the heartbeat of your business and driving your strategy?
- Which driving force do you think each of your key subordinates would *say* drives your company and acts as the strategic heartbeat of the business?

Our experience shows that when we pose these questions to a management team, there will be as many responses as there are people in the room at the time. Different people have different views as to what area of the business is propelling it forward and is the key determinant of the company's products, customers, and markets. Unfortunately, if there is lack of consensus and clarity around this key concept, the organization will zigzag its way forward.

Another set of key questions to pose once management has agreed (and getting agreement is not an easy task) about what is *currently* driving the business are these:

- What component of the business *should* drive the strategy of the business in the future?

- Should we continue to be driven as we have been, or should we explore another driving force?

- If we explore a new driving force, which one should that be?

- What implications will that have on the choices that we make on the nature of products, customers, and markets that we do or do not offer?

- What will our future strategic profile look like if we change the driving force of our company?

Assessing Strategic Fit. If the driving force of a company is not entirely clear, we can still assess strategic fit by asking the following questions.

Questions: Strategic Fit

- How similar are the products this opportunity brings compared to the products we currently offer?

- How similar are the markets (segments or geographic) this opportunity brings compared to the markets we currently serve?

- How similar are the customers this opportunity brings compared to the customers we currently serve?

- How similar are the production capabilities and/or processes this opportunity brings compared to the production capabilities we currently have?

- How similar is the technology this opportunity needs compared to the technology we currently know?

- How similar are the sales/marketing methods this opportunity requires compared to the ones we currently use?

- How similar are the distribution/delivery methods this opportunity requires compared to the ones we use currently?

- How similar are the human resources and skills this opportunity requires compared to those we have currently?
- How will the size/growth and return/profit criteria compare to our current levels of achievement?

Checklist: Strategic Fit

Product/service

Customer base

Market served

Technology/know-how

Production capacity/capability

Method of sales/marketing

Distribution method or system

Natural resources

Size/growth

Return/profit

The more similarity there is in each of the above areas, the closer the strategic fit. The more dissimilar the more remote the fit.

One can now add the strategic fit criterion to the assessment grid (see Figure 4-3).

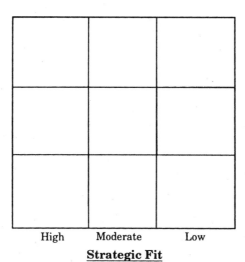

High   Moderate   Low
Strategic Fit

Figure 4-3. Strategic fit assessment grid. (*Copyright by Decision Processes International. All rights reserved.*)

Difficulty of Implementation. The fourth criterion is *difficulty of implementation*. Again, we have seen many good opportunities fail because management had simply understated the degree of difficulty in trying to capitalize on an opportunity.

The relative ease or difficulty of implementation really refers to the "organizational immune system" that every company seems to possess. We've seen numerous cases of good ideas that presented high benefit at reasonable cost, within the organization's strategic framework, but were rejected by this immune system.

A contemporary case in point is Honda's marketing of its new Acura automobiles. These cars represented Honda's entry into the luxury auto marketplace. Honda made a decision at the outset that these luxury cars could not be sold through the same dealerships that were handling the rest of the Honda line. It was apparently felt that the Honda "sales culture" would not be conducive to selling these high-end automobiles. So Honda's decision was to market these new cars only in separate dealerships, and even then, only in separate dealerships that maintained a certain physical distance from any nearby Honda dealerships. This decision was taken even at the risk of offending current Honda dealers. Honda clearly believed that its organizational immune system was not ready for luxury auto.

Even IBM, with all its success in the mainframe business, had some initial difficulties when it entered the PC field. The reasons were obvious. The customer base was not the same. Mainframes are sold to companies, PCs to individuals. Thus, the selling and distribution methods were different, and IBM had no experience selling directly to consumers.

The degree of difficulty encountered in introducing new products or entering new markets is directly proportionate to the number of changes that the organization will need to make from its current modus operandi. The more changes, the greater the degree of difficulty; the fewer changes, the less difficulty.

To assess the degree of implementation difficulty, the following question needs to be asked: *How much change will be required, in each of the following areas, to implement this new product or market opportunity?*

Checklist: Implementation Difficulty

Organization structure

Processes and/or systems

Skills and/or talents

Manufacturing methods and capabilities

Selling and/or marketing methods

Distribution or delivery methods

Technologies

Capital and financing

Legal and regulatory issues

Image, reputation, and quality

Compensation systems

Raw materials

Customer services

Corporate culture

Once the changes have been identified, the element that will determine the degree of difficulty is the amount of control the implementators have over those changes. The more control, the less the difficulty; the less control, the greater the difficulty. Another key question then, is: *How much control do we have over each of the changes we will need to make in our current modus operandi to implement this opportunity?*

Once these questions have been answered, then the degree of implementation difficulty can be assessed on the grid in Figure 4-4.

When we superimpose the cost-benefit grid over the strategic fit and

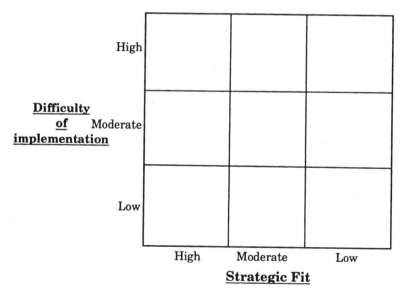

Figure 4-4. Difficulty of implementation and strategic fit assessment grid. (*Copyright by Decision Processes International. All rights reserved.*)

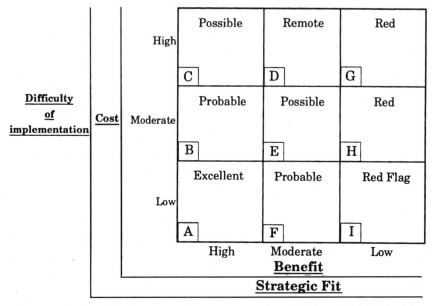

difficulty of implementation grid (Figure 4-5), we now have an objective ranking of the potential of each opportunity under review.

Interpreting the Assessment Grid

Certain conclusions can now be drawn. Obviously, an opportunity that falls in quadrant A on all four criteria is the best we will find: low in cost, high in benefit, good in strategic fit, and easy to implement. There are none better. Opportunities in quadrants B and F are probable. B quadrant opportunities are characterized by higher costs and more difficult implementation. Quadrant F opportunities are starting to stray from the strategy of the business and bring less benefit. Quadrant C opportunities bring very high costs together with a high difficulty of implementation. The opportunities in quadrants G, H, and I obviously are risky because they violate most of the four criteria.

Presented with such an assessment, the leader of an organization should use it to read the thought process of subordinates. For example, if an opportunity falls in quadrant D (but something about that opportunity attracts you to it), the grid specifies exactly what must be done to the opportunity before it can be pursued.

First, a way must be found to make it fit the strategy of the business (a move to the left). Second, ways must be found to reduce the costs (one or two moves down). Third, ways must be found to decrease the difficulty of implementation (one or two moves down). If we can affect these three variables, we can move the opportunity to quadrant A, and it will become viable. If not, it should be left where it is.

By examining the opportunity assessment ranking system, we can see that there are five possibilities for opportunities appearing in one or two of the nine boxes of the assessment grid. We have keyed these five possibilities by letter. The A box of the grid represents what are obviously the best opportunities. Cost is low while benefit is high, implementation is fairly easy, and strategic fit is high. This is the best of all possible worlds, and any opportunities finishing in the box after both sets of assessments should definitely by carried over to the next step of the process, opportunity development.

The B and F boxes represent probable opportunities. They would provide reasonable benefit, with reasonable cost. They fit well enough into the organization's direction and can be implemented without too much difficulty. These are opportunities that will require fine-tuning but should almost always be pursued and taken to the next step.

The C and E boxes represent possible opportunities. Cost might have to be reduced and implementation made easier. Some improvement in strategic fit will be needed. Possible opportunities need more than fine-tuning; they require some careful work. Nonetheless, they may still be excellent candidates for developing further.

The D box represents a remote opportunity. By *remote*, we mean you'd better have a very good reason for deciding to develop it further. Costs are high, and benefits are moderate. Although strategic fit is moderate, ability to implement will be strained. Remote opportunities are usually long shots, which, of course, can occasionally pay off. But if you decide to develop them, you need to do it with your eyes open to the attendant risks. The next step, development, will be crucial.

Boxes G, H, and I, the entire right side of the grid, are red flags. These are not opportunities, no matter how good they might have looked emerging from the search step. Threats are too high, benefits are too weak, the fit is too forced. We find that the chances of shipwreck are all too high for those who attempt to sail in these waters. The ideas that ended up in these boxes are worse than a remote possibility, which could at least be managed to a more favorable outcome. These are strictly gambles, rolls of the dice; they are highly dangerous.

As a result of applying the assessment grid to all the opportunities, the best ones—like cream—will migrate to the top. These are the ones that we now want to take through the final two steps of the product or market innovation process.

5

Opportunity Development: Getting to "la Crème de la Crème"

In the 1960s, Ford introduced a new car called the Skyliner which was truly a new-to-the-market concept. The main feature was a removable hardtop that could be stored in the trunk of the car. In spite of all the advertising the company bought to introduce it, the free press the car received because of its novelty, and all the favorable reviews the car got from car magazines and editors, the product was a miserable failure.

In the early 1990s, largely as a result of Dell Computer's unexpected success, Digital Equipment (DEC) decided to sell its PCs direct to consumers. The attempt was a miserable failure.

In 1987, American Express, the powerhouse of the plastic card industry, introduced a new card called Optima to compete directly with VISA and Mastercard. Two years later, the company had $1.5 billion of unpaid charges. The product was a miserable failure.

However, Bass, the United Kingdom's largest brewer, has just introduced a new product—an ale called Caffey's—that is surpassing all their expectations. Its first year's sales will be over 100,000 barrels, twice what the company expected.

Why is it that some new product introductions have soaring success while others fail miserably? The reason, in our view, is that one company has taken its opportunity through a step we call *development* but the other has not.

In the assessment step, each new product opportunity was placed under a floodlight; in the development step, each new product opportunity will be placed under a spotlight, to be examined in more depth and detail than in the previous step.

New product introductions succeed or fail based on management's ability to anticipate the *critical factors* that will deliver one or the other result. The development step is the *transition* to the formal pursuit, or introduction, of the new opportunity. It is the organization's ability to *think* through the implementation *before* it implements.

In the case of the Skyliner, Ford did not anticipate the reaction of the customer to a car without trunk space. After all, if the hardtop goes into the trunk, where does the trunk go? Where will I put my belongings when I go on long trip with the top down on a beautiful, warm sunny day? All these questions could have been answered in advance of the launch through a short customer survey but obviously were not, and that failure led to the new product's demise.

DEC underestimated the degree of difficulty required to acquire or develop the direct response selling and delivery skills that Dell had mastered. In fact, DEC attempted to clone Dell's strategic capabilities and were unable to do so, a technique not recommended by us and which will be discussed in more depth in the next chapter.

As far as the Optima disaster is concerned, Amex also did not anticipate a critical factor when introducing a new card which allowed its holder credit, something Amex had never done before. Unlike its previous cards, where the holder is expected to pay the instant the monthly statement arrives, a credit card allows the holder a time relapse or to pay only a part of the total. Furthermore, most holders also want a "grace" period to pay the remainder. Again, this critical factor could have been anticipated and managed successfully. However, Amex ignored this vital element of success, and the new product turned out to be a major failure.

Best-Case and Worst-Case Scenarios

The first part of the development step is to construct scenarios. In other words, management must try to foresee what would be the best possible set of outcomes for the new opportunity as well as the worst possible set of outcomes for that same opportunity. These scenarios can be captured in the following format.

Each opportunity, starting with the best one first, is now examined, and best- and worst-case scenarios are constructed using the results we could expect if we were to pursue this opportunity. The following are the development questions to ask:

Process Questions

- Best-case scenario: If we pursued this opportunity, what are all the best results this opportunity would bring?

- Worst-case scenario: If we pursued this opportunity, what are all the worst results this opportunity would bring?

The results can be listed on an opportunity development worksheet (see Figure 5-1).

OPPORTUNITY DEVELOPMENT WORKSHEET

Opportunity/Concept: _____

WORST-CASE SCENARIO YIELD/PRODUCTIVITY	BEST-CASE SCENARIO YIELD/PRODUCTIVITY

Figure 5-1.

Risk-Reward Relationship

After the construction of best-case and worst-case scenarios, we can bring into the process another powerful filter. That filter is to examine the relationship between *risk* and *reward*. The purpose of the risk-reward analysis is to measure the positive or negative impact each new product or market opportunity could have relative to the status quo. Here are the questions to ask about risk and reward:

Process Questions

- Compared to where we are now (the status quo), where will the best-case scenario take us?

- Compared to where we are now (the status quo), where will the worst-case scenario take us?

The scale to use in answering the process questions is shown in Figure 5-2. A variety of permutations and combinations can result as a firm answers these two questions; here are a few possibilities:

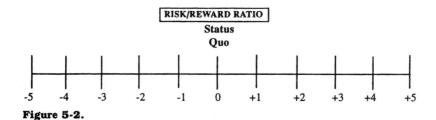

Figure 5-2.

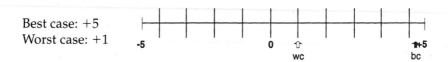

Best case: +5
Worst case: +1

Conclusion: No risk. Even if we achieve only the worst-case results, we will be better off than we are today.

Best case: +1
Worst case: −5

Conclusion: High risk. There is much more to lose than there is to gain. Is it worth the effort?

Best case: −1
Worst case: −5

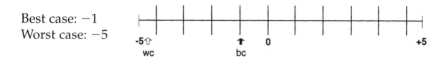

Conclusion: How can an opportunity, which is a good thing, take us back from the status quo? Sometimes it happens. A case in point is an opportunity our own firm explored a couple of years ago. One of our competitors, which was three times our size, became available for purchase. Obviously, this was an attractive opportunity, since we could have quadrupled our business overnight. However, that particular competitor came with a bad reputation in the marketplace, and we felt that we would acquire not only the competitor but its reputation as well. This we felt, would set us back from where we were (the status quo). We declined.

Best case: +3
Worst case: −2

Conclusion: If one factor falls on the plus side and the other on the minus side, we must look at the spread between the two. A (+1, −4) is obviously not as good as a (+4, −1).

The calibrations on the scale are unimportant. You can choose larger numbers, more numbers, or finer calibrations. What is important, however, is to maintain consistency in order to evaluate the gap that exists between the best case and the worst case, between risk and reward.

For purposes of consistency, the following definitions might be helpful.

- −5 equals disastrous results: business, jobs, morale, and/or image will all suffer severely; could represent failure of a small business, "black eye" for a large business; severe risk.

- −4 equals substantial risk: major disruptions to organization; money will be lost; recovery and return to normal operations will not be easy.

- −3 equals significant risk: remedial actions will have to be taken to restore situation; progress toward business goals will be disrupted; effects will be remembered and will have consequences for the future.

- −2 equals some risk, though it will seem to be controllable: within many organizations, would come under "freedom to fail" latitude; only those most directly affected will understand the setback, which will be considered minor.

- −1 equals very little risk: at worst, considered a minor snag; virtually no one will be aware of negative consequences; relatively little work will be necessary to restore status quo.

- 0 equals status quo; performance, morale, image, return, flexibility, and relationships will remain precisely as they are today.

- +1 equals slight improvement: most people will not even realize what has taken place; those directly affected will see a minor advantage; results will be short-lived, and quickly forgotten.

- +2 equals clear improvement: those most closely involved will be highly appreciative of the result; improvement will be tangible and repeatable.

- +3 equals significant improvement: entire organization will either use or be quickly aware of it; effects will be somewhat longer lived; considered a clear advance, which the organization will attempt to exploit.

- +4 equals dramatic improvement: clear competitive inroads and/ or operating efficiencies will result; long-term benefits; significant event for organization; will gain outside notice as well.

- +5 equals landmark improvement: turning point and/or watershed event in the development of the company and/or individual; improvement will launch company or department to leadership position; profound change on culture and/or operations of the organization.

General Observations Regarding the Risk-Reward Calibrations

Here are some recommendations for determining how to treat opportunities as evaluated on the risk-reward analysis scale and whether to carry them forward to the pursuit step. Naturally, these are ultimately your decisions, but these guidelines should be helpful in determining where your opportunities fall.

1. *Both best-case and worst-case scenarios rate a positive and are at least + 1 or above on the scale:* These opportunities should be taken to the pursuit step, without exception.

2. *Best- and worst-case scenarios range anywhere from −1 to +1:* These opportunities are seldom worth pursuing because they have minimal impact while requiring attention and focus to see them through correctly. (If they are not followed up on correctly, the negative impact could be much worse than projected.) Sometimes such opportunities can be delegated to others, to test the ability of subordinates to implement. Even in this case, however, you should be acutely aware of the time and energy investment as compared to the relatively small impact that will result.

3. *Best- and worst-case scenarios range from 0 to −5:* Obviously, these are not opportunities that should be pursued.

4. *Best case is +1 or less, and worst case is 0 or worse:* In general, do not pursue the opportunity.

5. *Opportunities whose positive number exceeds the negative number:* These are the best opportunities to pursue, for example, a +2 over a −1, a +3 over a −2, a +4 over a −3, a +5 over a −4, or, of course, a better relationship than any of these. A +5 over a −2, on one hand, is highly attractive; moving the negative number only two points to the left—creating a +5 over a −4—creates, on the other hand, an opportunity that carries the potential for severe risk. As we've stated earlier, the critical factors come into prominent play when you're dealing with opportunities that bridge the status quo.

6. *Opportunities that rate less than +2 or less than a −2:* If you seek to be very safe and conservative in seeking opportunity, never pursue one that rates less than a +2 or less than a −2. That is, the *best* case has to be at least +2, and the *worst* case can be no worse than −2.

7. *Worst-case scenarios that rate −4 or −5:* We recommend that you never pursue an opportunity that rates a −4 or −5 worst case—irrespective of the best case projection—unless you are clear on and confident of the critical factors that need to be addressed to mitigate the worst-case scenario.

The result of using risk-reward analysis is that we now can home in on the "crème de la crème" of opportunities. At the top of our list now are the very best of all the new product/market opportunities available.

Starting the Transition to Implementation

The second part of the development step is to start *thinking* about how we can achieve the best-case scenario while avoiding the worst-case scenario. In order to do this, we must now attempt to identify the *criti-*

cal factors that will lead to one or the other of the two scenarios. The following are questions to ask about critical factors:

Process Questions
- What critical factors will cause the worst-case scenario?
- What critical factors will cause the best-case scenario?

The critical factors that could cause either scenario are listed as follows:

Worst-Case Scenario   **Critical Factors/Likely Causes**

_____   _____

_____   _____

_____   _____

_____   _____

_____   _____

_____   _____

_____   _____

_____   _____

_____   _____

Best-Case Scenario   **Critical Factors/Likely Causes**

_____   _____

_____   _____

_____   _____

_____   _____

_____   _____

_____   _____

_____   _____

_____   _____

_____   _____

Some readers, at this stage, might be asking "What in the world is a critical factor?" Our answer: anything that would *cause* the best-case or worst-case scenario to happen. An example might be in order. A best-case scenario in terms of yield and productivity for a hypothetical company might took something like this:

- Market share gain from current 13 percent to estimated 16 percent
- Ability to cover northeast territory with 7 salespeople rather than 11
- Appeal to a user group, not currently being reached, estimated at 250,000 people

Examples of a worst-case scenario might be:

- No increase in current market share
- Reduction in salespeople covering northeast territory from 11 to no fewer than 9
- Estimated numbers on access to a user group not currently reached are unknown, but 50,000 would be the minimum

Having listed the outcomes that would produce the worst-case and best-case scenarios, you're now in a position to list the critical factors that will tend to bring about the best case and the critical factors that will tend to bring about the worst case. Using our example above, let's say that the critical factor that will enable us to reduce the number of salespeople in the northeast territory is the rapid assimilation of the new computerized ordering system by the top performers. The critical factor underlying our chance of gaining market share will be our ability to smoothly implement our new computerized ordering process before the competition does; in fact, our beating them to the punch, and the degree to which we do so, is the all-important factor in this area. The critical factor in reaching the 250,000 people who constitute a new user group is the acquisition of accurate mailing lists, which will help us determine where the users are and how to reach them.

The worst-case critical factors will sometimes be the converse of the best-case critical factors, but sometimes they will be quite different. For example, a critical factor in our inability to decrease the number of salespeople from 11 to any fewer than 9 might be the sales force's inability to rapidly assimilate the new computerized ordering system. Another critical factor in this area, however, might be the perception by the sales force that we are looking to replace all of them eventually; for this reason, they may be deliberately reluctant to use the new system to its maximum potential. A critical factor in our not being able to increase the market share might be our delay in introducing the new computer ordering system, thereby losing ground to the competition. It might, however, be a competitive action that offsets our early advantage.

In an attempt to help our clients better identify critical factors that contribute to the result of the best or worst outcomes, we have, over the years, developed the following checklist. The areas listed below, together with their subsets, are generally the key areas that bring about either scenario.

Critical Factors Checklist

Technical Factors

- Availability or requisite scientific/technical skills
- Adequacy of research resources
- Quality and quantity of support personnel
- Probability of technical success and validation
- Government and/or regulatory position

Timing Factors

- Research completion versus market need
- Market preparation and development
- Known and assumed competitive actions

Stability Factors

- Durability of the market
- Chances for a dominant or preeminent position
- Probability and impact of down markets
- Stability of largest projected users
- Volatility of the approach

Position Factors

- Impact on other products and services
- Impact on overall credibility
- Ability to assume a rapid leadership position
- Ability to facilitate other opportunities

Growth Factors

- Diversification

- Possibility of substantial future growth in volume, units, and/or revenue
- Possibility of a family of products
- Possibility of changes or shifts in the industry of which this product and/or service can take advantage
- Short-term market potential
- Long-term market potential
- Impact on market share

Marketability Factors

- Market potential in the immediate future
- Market potential in long-range future
- Compatibility with current and long-range marketing objectives
- Competitive environment
- Promotional requirements to launch
- Promotional requirements to sustain
- Adequacy of present distribution systems
- User view of cost versus value
- Applicability to current customers
- Servicing requirements
- Impact on reputation

Production Factors

- Capabilities of production facilities
- Utilization of familiar production processes
- Availability of human resources

Financial Factors

- Calculation of DCF
- Expected ROI
- Expected increase in profits or earnings per share
- Expected new capital outlays for equipment
- Expected cost to complete the project
- Expected cost to complete the development

Protection

- Possibility of a patent
- Unique character of the product, process, service

   Once an opportunity successfully negotiates the development step to your satisfaction, it's time to put the opportunity into practice. We established at the outset of this book that innovation can only be successful when it is implemented. Product concepts that aren't implemented aren't innovations. Consequently, we will also turn to the implementation of opportunities, which we call the *pursuit step*.

   After the identification of all the critical factors of success or failure is completed, we are now ready to proceed into the last, and final, step of new product or new market innovation—the launch.

6

Launching New Opportunities: The Pursuit Step

For an organization, it is as debilitating to ignore good opportunities as it is to implement bad ones. Consequently, we have found that the *pursuit step* is especially important in providing a systematic approach to recommendations as well as to implementation. This step is probably most important, however, for encouraging *risk management* and *risk containment*. We've established that innovative companies take prudent risk, not excessive risk. Opportunity pursuit enables you to objectively determine how much risk is present and what you can realistically do to minimize or eliminate it. Appropriate actions then become a part of the implementation.

The pursuit step takes us from *transitional thinking* into the world of *implementation*. For new product and/or market concepts to be successful, the implementors must concentrate on two key elements. One is containing or *preventing* the worst-case scenario from materializing and the other is assuring or *promoting* the best-case scenario. Thus the need, at this stage in the process, is to introduce the concepts of *preventive* and *promotive* actions.

Preventive and Promotive Actions

The pursuit step concentrates on taking special actions to remove obstacles to the effective implementation of the opportunity. This activity includes solving *potential problems*. The fundamental premise

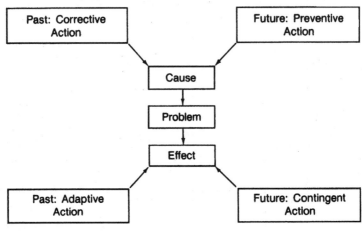

Figure 6-1.

in effective problem solving is a simple one: *You cannot remove a problem without removing its cause.* You can *adapt* to a problem's effects without knowing the cause, but you can never completely remove the problem unless you know the cause and take action against it. Similarly, you cannot *promote* an outcome without knowing *its* cause. Note that there are several variables to consider when deciding whether to take *adaptive* or *corrective* action. These variables include cost of the various actions, inconvenience caused by the actions, time available to take the actions, and ultimate severity of the effects on the innovator. When trying to avoid or mitigate future problems, we take preventive actions against causes and contingent actions against effects. "No smoking" signs are meant to prevent the cause of a fire (careless smoker), and sprinklers are intended to reduce the effects if the problem occurs (see Figure 6-1).

All these actions, however, deal with problem solving. Since we are talking about innovation and opportunity, we need to add two types of action to our list. Those actions are *promoting* and *exploiting* (see Figure 6-2).

Promoting actions also address causes and, like preventive actions, address those causes in the *future*. But if preventive actions seek to keep the cause of a problem from occurring, promoting actions seek to ensure that the cause of an opportunity *will* occur. There is nothing about innovation that should be left to chance. Consequently, as critical factors emerge that could spell the difference between the success or failure of an opportunity, it is important to promote those critical

Cause and Effect: Opportunities.

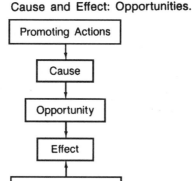

Figure 6-2.

factors that will cause the best possible outcome. Similarly, exploiting actions seek to maximize the benefit that is achieved from the effects of the opportunity. You might call this a *capitalizing* action. As contingent action seeks to mitigate the effects of some potential problem, exploiting action seeks to further stimulate the benefit from any of a potential opportunity's effects that may occur.

For example, with the deregulation of the telephone industry, many alternative publishing companies have started to produce their own yellow pages. At least one of the critical factors in the success of these alternative yellow pages is the inclusion of as many businesses and services as possible, so that the new book is seen as a viable alternative to the standard telephone company yellow pages. To promote the likelihood of this occurring, many of the alternative yellow pages publishers provided free listing for advertisers in the initial edition of their books. This was seen as a way to get as many businesses involved as possible and to demonstrate the credibility and utility of their books from the outset. This decision to provide free advertising in order to launch the books was a key *promoting* action. Still another promoting action was to provide the books for free in public places. Many publishers sought and received permission to provide displays with free copies in such places as local post offices. This greatly enhanced the distribution of the books and was another fundamental promoting action.

These actions were taken to stimulate use and to get the books into the hands of potential users. Now, what happens if the desired effect develops: People actively begin using the alternative yellow pages directory? Well, there should be several desirable and opportunistic effects. These effects will include applications for inclusion in the next printing of the book, the ability to charge competitive rates for future advertising, the credibility and financial support to expand circulation of the book into other communities, and the demonstrated usage that would justify outside financial support for expanded marketing activities. It's not sufficient, however, simply to sit back and wait for this to happen and to congratulate yourself if, indeed, it does. There should be plans in place—actions considered—that will exploit these positive effects of the opportunity. This is where exploiting actions enter the picture.

In our example, exploiting actions could include any of or all the following:

- Offering advertising contracts to future advertisers for periods of two, three, or more years at discounted rates.

- Establishing a modest charge for the book itself—a fee that would be tolerable to almost any user who is happy with the book, yet would help to defray some printing expenses

- Establishing a subscription service so that users could order yellow pages for those communities most useful to them at a reduced rate, thereby alerting potential advertisers to the demographic appeal of the book

In the pursuit step, we will therefore be carefully considering cause and effect and their relationships to our opportunity. That's why the development step raises critical factors specific to each opportunity that weren't necessary in the prior assessment step. The methodology is simple. You take each of the critical factors that were identified in the development step and you now identify actions that can either promote or prevent the critical factors. The accompanying worksheet might be helpful (Figure 6-3).

Obviously, the more promoting actions you develop, the higher the chances that the positive critical factor you want to occur will indeed occur. But when do you have enough? How much time is it worth to spend on developing these? Here are two quick guidelines:

1. The broader the range on the risk-reward analysis from the development step—the more the best case and worst case for the opportunity spans the status quo—the more time you should invest in being very careful in preventing the negative critical factors. The reason for this is that there is apparently a large downside risk.

2. You know from your intuition, experience, research, and/or perspective that a particular positive critical factor will mean the difference between success and failure. This is often a critical factor that has to do with organizational culture, politics, timing, or key positions in the hierarchy. You will want to surround that critical factor with promoting actions.

OPPORTUNITY PURSUIT WORKSHEET

OPPORTUNITY / CONCEPT: _____

Best-case scenario
yield / productivity

_____
_____
_____
_____
_____
_____
_____

Risk / Reward Ratio

Compared to the status quo, how much positive impact will the best case scenario have?

+ 5 — Landmark
+ 4 — Rare Opportunity
+ 3 — Significant Gain
+ 2 — Important Impact
+ 1 — Modest Gain

0 — Status Quo

Compared to the status quo, how much negative impact will the worst case scenario have?

- 1 — Modest Set Back
- 2 — Damage Control Needed
- 3 — Significant Set Back
- 4 — Highly Visible Failure
- 5 — Disaster

Worst-case scenario
yield / productivity

_____
_____
_____
_____
_____
_____
_____

Does this opportunity bring sufficient reward within acceptable risk to take to the next step? Yes _____ No _____

OPPORTUNITY PURSUIT WORKSHEET

List the critical factors that will cause "best-case" scenario:

_____
_____
_____
_____
_____

Promoting Actions
(To establish positive factors)

_____
_____
_____
_____
_____

List the critical factors that will cause "worst-case" scenario:

_____
_____
_____
_____
_____

Preventing Actions
(To discourage negative factors)

_____
_____
_____
_____
_____

Figure 6-3. (Copyright by Decision Processes International. All rights reserved.)

You may believe that some positive critical factors will happen with little or no help from you. For those factors, you might choose few or even no promoting actions, depending upon your confidence level. There is no one-to-one relationship between factors and actions. Some critical factors might receive one promoting action, others five or six. It all depends on your judgment, your perspective, and your knowledge of what has to be done. You should be able to see at this point, however, the importance of raising the critical issues during the best- and worst-case analysis that was performed in the development step. We think that this is a unique step in the product/market innovation process, one that tends to guarantee practical and realistic application of new concepts.

In a similar manner, you should turn to the negative critical factors, those that will tend to produce the worst-case scenario according to your work in the development step. For example, if a negative critical factor is budget constraint, then a *preventing action* might be an investigation of where money can be found in a "fat" part of the budget, that is, an area that won't produce the kind of productivity and yield gains that your opportunity will.

Building the Implementation Plan

Opportunity pursuit is the process of formulating an implementation plan and then beginning the actual implementation of opportunities. It relies heavily on the critical factors that were raised in the development step. It is a step that is specifically designed to focus on individual opportunities and to bridge the gap between the *conceptualization* and the *actualization* of these opportunities.

Opportunity pursuit makes innovation happen by allowing you to analyze those factors that will determine success or failure for your opportunity and by assigning *specific* actions that will help to enhance success and avoid failure. Pursuit is begun "on paper"—before energy, resources, and reputations have been committed. Once the plan takes a coherent shape, implementation begins. Although opportunity pursuit is not an absolute guarantee of success, it does function as an insurance policy, one designed to provide the greatest protection for you and your plan.

This brings us to the second part of the pursuit step, which is the pursuit plan itself. We have emphasized that we favor a simple, uncluttered, and orderly approach to this planning. You may wish, however, to incorporate the planning tools that you have found to be most effective or that your organization requires. We are not suggesting that there is anything unique or ideal about our particular planning format. We do feel, however, that it demonstrates the simplicity with which an opportunity can be planned and implemented. As we move from search, through assessment, through development, and finally to pursuit, we feel that the process should not become more and more complex, especially since at this point the opportunity might well involve people and departments who were not involved from the beginning of the innovation process. Therefore, it is even more essential that the work that has taken place up to this point is configured in a way that makes it readily understandable, easily communicated, and quickly summarized.

As you can see in the worksheet (Figure 6-4) and checklist that follow, the items listed under "Plan Steps" can be as detailed as you wish. The amount of detail will depend on which of the planning purposes you have in mind: a plan for the implementation of a specific opportunity; a plan for implementation that is to be made part of a larger plan; a tactical, management implementation document; or a guide to develop further information. We've seen many instances where plan steps, when circulated to those responsible, form the basis of a new pursuit plan worksheet for *each* of those individuals. For example, if one step in the plan is "notification to all retail dealers of a new discounting policy," the individual responsible for that step might in turn create substeps and target dates within that step.

Once again, we have found it useful to provide our clients with a "generic" checklist to help them prepare plans to introduce and pursue a new product/market opportunity:

Pursuit Action Plan Checklist

PLAN STEPS

- Prepare development plans
- Conduct feasibility studies/project definition
- Obtain program approval/funding
- Update development plans
- Implement marketing survey
- Develop test prototype
- Market-test, get customer feedback
- Revise product
- Engineer production
- Run first production run
- Test market
- Improve product

- Implement full production
- Distribute product
- Market
- Advertise/promote

NEW PRODUCT / MARKET PURSUIT

Opportunity: _____

Owner: _____

Plan Steps	Completion Date	Responsible	Contributors
1.			
2.			
3.			
4.			
5.			
6.			
7.			
8.			
9.			
10.			
11.			
12.			
13.			
14.			
15.			
16.			
17.			
18.			
19.			
20.			
21.			
22.			
23			
24.			
25.			

Figure 6-4. (*Copyright by Decision Processes International. All rights reserved.*)

Different Uses of the Pursuit Plan

There are at least four possible applications of the opportunity pursuit plan. First, the pursuit plan can become the actual implementation plan for a specific opportunity. This usually occurs when you are dealing with an opportunity that is completely within your ability to authorize and implement. In such a case, the pursuit plan is quite detailed and becomes the working document that you and your colleagues use to implement the opportunity.

When an opportunity must fit into a larger planning process (for example, one division's new product must fit into a larger corporate plan), the second application of the pursuit plan is to raise the key issues and actions that will become components of that larger plan. Those responsible for pursuing the opportunity are provided with a methodology to ensure that their interests are protected as the larger planning process evolves.

The pursuit plan can also serve as a tactical management tool that enables you to intelligently manage your resources and people. Specific attention is paid to the responsibilities and dates set in the opportunity pursuit step. This tactical plan is reviewed frequently by all concerned in the project to monitor progress and identify emerging trouble spots that were not considered earlier; the plan also serves as a fail-safe mechanism to safeguard the implementation as much as possible.

The fourth way to use the opportunity pursuit process is to highlight the fact that key information is missing or that actions deemed possible in the assessment and development steps are, in fact, not feasible. Although it is not the primary purpose of the pursuit step to serve as yet another filter in the innovation process, we have found that by its very nature of forcing people to identify specific actions and consider specific resources it can cause last-minute reconsideration of opportunities that are going from paper to action. Perhaps most powerfully, the disciplined, ordered, and systematic process that the opportunity pursuit step provides serves as a very powerful recommending tool because it places the implementation in a visible, objective, and documented format.

It is in this manner that a general pursuit plan is turned into individual elements and actions and, most important, is assigned to specific people to make sure that things get done. This is the core of effective implementation. Nothing can "fall through the slats" if specific responsibilities are assigned and clear completion dates are agreed on. As progress meetings take place, they should revolve around these pursuit planning worksheets so that attention remains focused on what was accomplished, by whom, on what dates, and what needs to be done in a similar fashion in the future. This allows for adjustments and contingencies to be included in the plan as it evolves. Opportunity pursuit should be an organic and dynamic process, changing as implementation moves forward and adapting to new conditions as necessary.

The two elements that *must* be a part of the plan steps, however, are the promoting and preventing actions from the previous worksheet. This is the finalization of the bridge from the development step to implementation in that critical factors are being addressed through the inclusion of their appropriate promoting and preventing actions as a part of the planning process. These actions may be the heart of the implementation process, because they are the key to ensuring the critical factors that will tend to promote success and to mitigate or eliminate the critical factors that will tend to hinder success. Consequently, if you see target dates missed, responsibilities shirked, and progress generally missing at key checkpoints, you know immediately that you must regroup—implementation is going awry. Without these important actions being carefully considered and included in the plan, the best innovations—despite their relative benefit and appeal—rise and fall on nothing more than the roll of the dice that we tried to avoid from the outset of the innovation process.

Beware of Change Resisters!

The greatest risk to the failure of a well-conceived plan, in our experience, doesn't come from outside the organization but rather from inside. And the greatest potential problem to the successful implementation is what we have come to call "change resisters." Because new product/market opportunities stem from some change, many people do not like change, and overcoming their anxiety is the implementor's greatest challenge. Machiavelli said it best (*The Prince*, Penguin Books):

> It must be remembered that there is nothing more difficult to plan, more doubtful of success, not more dangerous to manage than the creation of a new system. For the initiator has the enmity of all who would profit by the preservation of the old institution and merely lukewarm defenders in those who would gain by the new ones.
>
> And let it be noted that there is no more delicate matter to take in hand, nor more dangerous to conduct, nor more doubtful in its success, than to set up as a leader in the introduction of changes. For he who innovates will have for his enemies all those who are well off under the existing order of things, and only lukewarm supporters in those who might be better off under the new.

This lukewarm temper arises partly from the fear of adversaries who have the laws on their side, and partly from the incredulity of mankind, *who will never admit the merit of anything new, until they have seen it proved by the event.* The result, however, is that when the enemies of change make an attack, they do so with all the zeal of partisans, while the others defend themselves so feebly as to endanger both themselves and their cause.

Since we view innovation as "creative destruction" of the status quo, it is easy to understand why people who benefit from the status quo are threatened by it. However, there is no alternative to progress. Change can be made less threatening to people if it is accompanied by a conscious and visible process.

7

Leveraging Your Product Innovation Investment

As we worked with more and more companies over the years, we noticed that some got much more "bang for the buck" from their product development efforts than others. For example, why is it that Merck can develop 12 new blockbuster prescription drugs in a 10-year period when the industry average is 1 every 15 years?

The answer is simple. Those that outperformed their competitors in product innovation had clearly identified the *driving force* at the root of their strategy and had also clearly identified the corresponding *strategic capabilities* that the companies must excel at to make their strategies succeed over their competitors.

Over time, the strategy of an organization, like a person, can become stronger and healthier or it can get weaker and sicker. In our opinion, what determines which way the strategy will go are the *areas of excellence* that a company *deliberately cultivates* over time to keep the strategy strong and healthy and give it an edge in the marketplace. An area of excellence is a *describable skill, competence,* or *capability* that a company cultivates to a level of proficiency greater than anything else it does and particularly better than any competitor does. It is excellence in these two or three key areas that keeps its strategy alive and working. Bill Marriott, of the hotel chain, stated in *Fortune* magazine that "it took the company over a decade to figure out that it had special expertise in running hospitality and food-service operations." This "special expertise" or capability is what we call *an area of excellence* or *strategic capability*.

The reason for Merck's success stems from ex-CEO Ray Vagelos's deliberate investment in four areas of medical science—namely, biochemistry, neurology, immunology, and molecular biology. All 12 of the blockbuster drugs derived from these four strategic capabilities deliberately cultivated by Vagelos to a higher level of proficiency than any of its competitors.

Thus, our advice to our clients is that the best product innovation is one that *leverages upon the company's strategic capabilities* and "fits" the strategy of the business.

We have also discovered that a company that attempts to innovate outside its strategic parameters (its driving force and accompanying areas of excellence), usually fails. And there is yet another good reason for that to occur: Most innovations *stem from prior knowledge.*

For example, it is not a coincidence that Edison and Siemens invented the light bulb, in different parts of the world, within hours of each other. Neither man would have done this if electricity and the conduction of electricity through wire had not been invented first. Mr. Daimler and Mr. Benz would not have discovered the automobile if the combustion engine had not been discovered first. Steve Jobs and Steve Wozniak would not have developed the personal computer if someone else had not discovered the microprocessor first. And the list goes on.

Proof of this notion is Leonardo da Vinci. As brilliant a new product innovator as he was—he conceived the bicycle, the helicopter, and the submarine over 400 years ago—the fact remains that most of his ingenious inventions never saw the light of day. One cannot build a helicopter without the prior knowledge of shaping flat metal. One cannot build a submarine without the prior knowledge of providing oxygen to a vehicle submerged underwater.

The same is true in a company. Every company develops areas of knowledge and expertise that it adds to over time, and any new product innovation that draws on that knowledge has a high probability of success, whereas any that does not has a high probability of failure.

Thus, a company can leverage its new product innovation investment by favoring innovations that draw on the strategic heartbeat (driving force) and the accompanying strategic capabilities (areas of excellence) of the enterprise. In fact, *leveraging these across the broadest array of products and markets* is the key to a product innovation program that will outspace the competition.

Too often organizations are distracted from what has made them successful. The most successful organizations are the ones where the leader and senior management clearly understand their driving force and fuel the key areas of excellence required for success with more resources each year than they give to other areas. They then pursue this strategy with total dedication and without allowing any competitor to attain the same level of excellence in those few key capabilities. As Benjamin Disraeli so clearly noted many decades ago, "The secret to success is constancy of purpose." And as the CEO of J. P. Morgan, one of the world's most successful banks, said about the firm he heads: "We aren't likely to deviate radically from the clear strategic path we have been on since the days of the first Morgan partners."

Sometimes, an area of excellence or strategic capability is one that has been cultivated over a long period of time. Pioneer, the Iowa corn seed king, dominates its rivals because it has deliberately cultivated the skill of gene juggling to a higher level of proficiency than any competitor. The company develops more than 20,000 hybrids per year, of which only 5 to 10 make it to market. And it has been doing this for over 65 years. The result has been an increase in farmers' yields from 40 to 110 bushels an acre.

Knowing what strategic area drives your organization and the corresponding areas of excellence required to support that strategy is akin to understanding what the strategic weapon is that will give you a distinct and sustainable advantage in the marketplace. Our experience has clearly shown that any strategy can work but that no company can pursue two strategies simultaneously. No organization has the resources to develop excellence in several areas concurrently.

Understanding the concepts of strategic drive or driving force and areas of excellence makes life for the CEO and the management team much easier in terms of the decisions they make about new products, markets, and customers that constitute the future profile of the organization.

Corporate or Business Unit Innovation?

"Corporations don't compete, business units do." So says Michael Porter of the Harvard Business School in his book *Competitive Advantage* (Free Press, 1985). This conclusion is based on the notion that as a company grows into an array of multiple products and customer groups, it ends up in a variety of different markets, each with a different group of competitors. Thus the need, and the Porter rationale, to separate the corporation into business units based on a product/customer matrix that places each unit "closer to the market" and increases its ability to compete successfully.

In our view, nothing could be further from the truth. Our own experience with all 300 of our clients clearly indicates the opposite phenomenon. It is *companies* that compete and not business units! In fact, what will determine a business unit's ability to compete (or not compete) is determined even before that business unit is formed.

The Link between Business Unit Success and Corporate Competitiveness

Successful companies, in our view, are those that can *leverage their unique set of capabilities (driving force and areas of excellence) across the largest number of products and markets.* Companies that can spread the heartbeat of the business and their accompanying strategic capabilities across as many business units as possible are those that will assist that business unit in surviving and prospering. The opposite is also true. Business units that cannot use key corporate capabilities are often "orphaned" from the thrust of the corporation and will have difficultly making it on their own.

Examples abound. Unfortunately, most are from Japan, because business unit competition seems to be a concept that Japanese companies understand much better than their U.S. counterparts. Sharp, of Japan, is an excellent example. Sharp is into LCDs for laptop computers as well as a large number of other consumer electronic devices from cordless phones, projection televisions, and fax machines to elec-

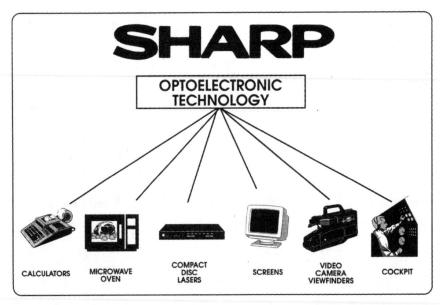

Figure 7-1. (*Copyright by Decision Processes International. All rights reserved.*)

tronic diaries and calculators. It has recently introduced laser diodes for use in computers, laser printers, CD players, and videodisc players. It is working on photosensitive films that will someday function as a self-contained image-processing computer and eliminate the need for memory chips and microprocessors. Why is Sharp engaged in all these diverse product, customer, and market areas? They all draw on Sharp's knowledge of optoelectronic technology (see Figure 7-1). "We've been accumulating optoelectronics know-how for 21 years" says President Haruo Tsuji in a *Business Week* article, which accounts for Sharp's success as the world's largest supplier of optoelectronic devices with sales of over $11 billion yearly. Sharp, in our opinion, has mastered this concept to the nth degree. Figure 7-2 is a "family tree" that shows over 250 products that stem from Sharp's superior expertise in the area of liquid crystal displays.

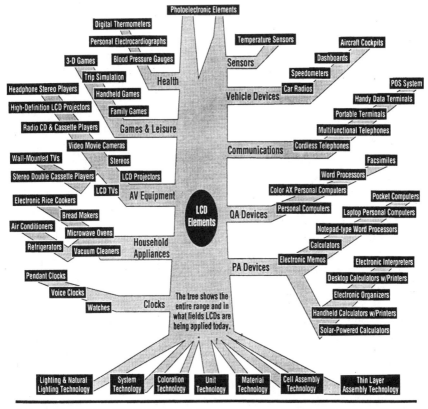

SHARP'S EXPANDING WORLD OF LIQUID CRYSTAL DISPLAYS (LCDs)

Figure 7-2.

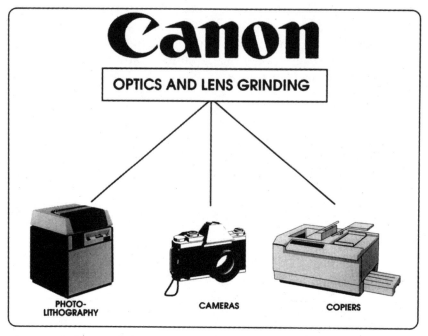

Figure 7-3. (*Copyright by Decision Processes International. All rights reserved.*)

Canon and Casio are two more Japanese examples. Canon's wide range of products—copiers, cameras, and fax machines—all draw on that company's imaging and microprocessor know-how (see Figure 7-3). Canon is also a good example of what happens when a company tries to innovate outside its strategic capabilities. In the mid-1980s, Canon made an enormous investment in the fast-growing and seductive PC market by introducing a PC of its own. Massive investment, massive failure. Why? Have you ever seen a PC with a lens? No lens, no probability of success. However, if Canon could ever figure out how to design a PC with a lens that makes it do things other PCs can't, then it would probably have a winner.

The calculators, television screens, watches, and musical instruments that come from Casio all have the common trait of drawing on the company's expertise in the areas of semiconductors and digital displays (see Figure 7-4).

A fifth Japanese company that clearly understands its heartbeat (driving force) is Honda. Although its most visible products are its cars, Honda also makes lawn mowers, motorcycles, and generators (Figure 7-5). All these products revolve around Honda's key expertise—engines—and the company is religiously following Honda's

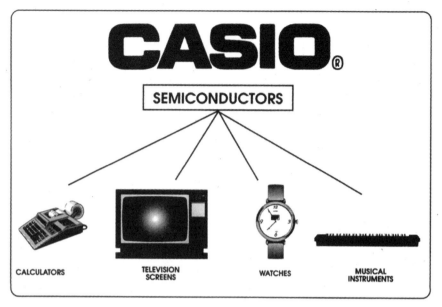

Figure 7-4. (*Copyright by Decision Processes International. All rights reserved.*)

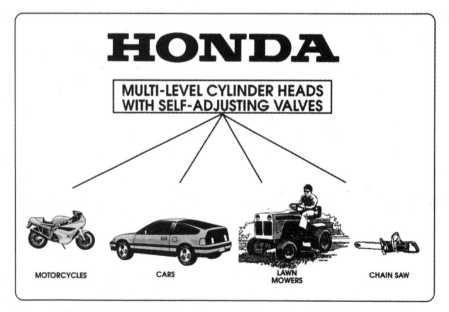

Figure 7-5. (*Copyright by Decision Processes International. All rights reserved.*)

business concept of "engines for the world." When Honda entered Formula 1 racing, it went in with its engines. The car bodies were by McLaren, Lotus, and others.

Canada's Northern Telecom is another company that clearly understands its strategic capability and has been exploiting it very successfully worldwide for a number of years. When Northern Telecom developed the software for its first digital switch, it did so in a manner to ensure that it would be used in a wide range of products including hybrid analog switches, configured central office switches, and PBXs (see Figure 7-6).

The news is not all bad for U.S. companies. Some clearly know where their strategic advantage lies. Hewlett-Packard and 3M are two good examples. Hewlett-Packard has exploited its knowledge of instrumentation technology into everything from scientific measuring devices to oscilloscopes (see Figure 7-7).

3M is probably the best U.S. example as a company that has built an array of more than 50,000 products based on its knowledge of polymer chemistry as applied to coatings and adhesives. This strategic capability has led 3M into some 50 business arenas such as film, floppy disks, videocassettes, audiotape, sandpaper, adhesive tape, electrical tape, computer wires—to their most recent success, Post-it Notes (see Figure 7-8).

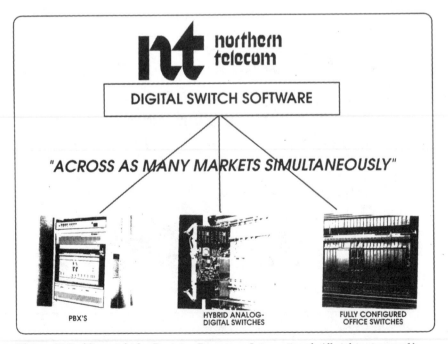

Figure 7-6. (*Copyright by Decision Processes International. All rights reserved.*)

Figure 7-7. (*Copyright by Decision Processes International. All rights reserved.*)

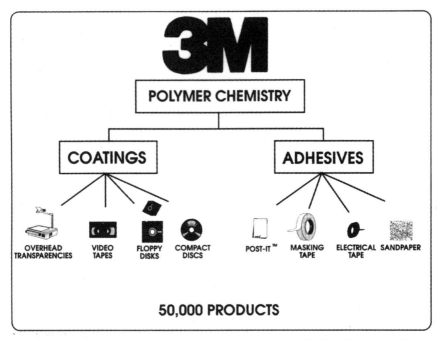

Figure 7-8. (*Copyright by Decision Processes International. All rights reserved.*)

Another CEO who clearly understands his company's strategic heartbeat and its corresponding area of excellence, and the advantage of leveraging these across all products and markets, is Percy Barnevik of ABB, the electrical equipment company based in Switzerland. Although the company sells locomotives, robotics, turbines, and power generation equipment, at the root of all these businesses is ABB's expertise in electricity and electronics—a technology-based strategy. As such, Barnevik fuels and cultivates that expertise by investing 8 percent, as compared to 5 percent by competitors, into R&D. "You have to be in command of your core technology," he says in an article appearing in *Fortune*. "For us, it's power semiconductors (electronic switching devices for high-voltage transmission), and I wouldn't dream of buying them from the Japanese." He then ensures that this capability is spread across all of ABB's businesses, which is the leverage that the corporate parent brings to each of its business units.

There are also some examples of companies that do not understand what is at the root of their business. In the late 1970s and early 1980s Armco, up to that time a very successful steel company, decided to diversify. And diversify it did! Into everything from oil rigs, petroleum exploration, building products, strategic metals, and insurance. For a short time, the new strategy seemed to pay off with record profits. But in 1982 the company lost $342 million, and it is still trying to recuperate to this day. The reason: When these unrelated businesses got into trouble, Armco management, who were steel people, did not understand the unrelated businesses, and Armco itself was not bringing any strategic advantage to any of them.

Another example is United Airlines. Under its previous CEO, United negotiated cost-reduction labor contracts with its unions only to use the money to diversify into hotel and car rentals with its purchase of Hertz and Hilton—two businesses to which it brought little advantage. Even the union executive, Captain Jim Damron, understood this, when, in a *Business Week* article, he complained: "In two consecutive contracts, we gave concessions to the company, and we received nothing in exchange except seeing our company lose 25 percent of our market share. They took that economic leverage and used it to buy hotels and rental cars."

The lesson to be learned from all these examples is quite clear. The CEO and the management team must clearly understand what is the driving force of the business that constitutes its strategic weapon and competitive advantage. As one Exxon executive told this author about why Exxon eventually retreated from its disastrous foray into office equipment: "We did not understand the 'trivia' of those businesses and, therefore, could bring nothing to the table."

Strategic Leverage

Understanding what component of the business is its strategic heartbeat and what are your company's strategic capabilities will greatly enhance your ability to succeed in your current markets, as well as open up other opportunities in possibly unrelated product/market areas that are strategically sound because they draw on the firm's strategic heartbeat and areas of excellence.

Honda recently announced the development of a new car engine that meets the 1998 California emission standards today—without the need to change anything about the gasoline. How long do you think it will be before Honda introduces this technology into its lawn mowers, chain saws, and tractors? Right! 12.5 seconds! Why? Simply because the competitive position of each of these business units will be enhanced by drawing on this corporate capability.

Strategic leverage means changing the equation that says that $1 + 1 = 2$ into one that says that $1 + 1 = 3$, sometimes 4 and sometimes 5. Decisions that affect only one product, one customer group, or one geographic area keep the organization running in place. To grow faster than competitors, one must make decisions and investments that enhance the competitiveness of multiple products, multiple customers, and multiple geographic markets, *simultaneously!*

Two other CEOs that understand this concept extremely well are Michael Eisner of Walt Disney and Ted Turner of Turner Broadcasting. Turner has built a number of cable networks that utilize each other's programs. A news piece seen on *Prime News* on Tuesday evening is seen again on *The International Hour* on Saturday afternoon and then seen at some other time on *CNN Headline News*—a separate network. It eventually makes its way across all the Turner networks such as The Airport Channel in airport gate areas to The Worldwide Hotel Channel in hotel rooms around the world.

At Disney, Michael Eisner has done the same type of leveraging to increase Disney's revenues from a few hundred million when he took over to over $8 billion 10 years later. His leveraging concept is simple: Start with a character—Aladdin—and produce an animated film. Then leverage that character across a number of other products and markets. First, you have Aladdin look-alikes greet customers at Disneyland and Disney World. Then you sell Aladdin dolls at these parks plus in all Disney stores around the country. Then you show the film on your own Disney cable network. Then you license the Aladdin character for a host of other uses from coloring books to hats and T-shirts. Finally you sell a video version through video stores such as Blockbuster. And the business grows exponentially!

The essence of a successful product innovation program, therefore, is the CEO's and management's clear understanding of which component of the business is more important than all others and is the heartbeat of the business—and, as such, lends itself more to certain products, customers, market segments, and geographic markets.

Determining the Strategic Capabilities of the Business

The deliberate cultivation of strategically important capabilities, usually two or three of them, keeps an organization's strategy strong and healthy and gives it an edge over its competitors. Losing these two or three skills weakens the strategy and eliminates the organization's competitive edge. Depending on which of the 10 driving forces is being pursued, the areas of excellence required to succeed will greatly change.

Product/Service Concept–Driven Strategy

A product/service concept–driven company survives on the *quality* of its product or service. Witness the automobile wars. Who's winning? The Japanese. Why are Americans buying Japanese cars and even willing to pay premium prices for them during this period of quota restrictions? The answer is simple: The Japanese make better cars. The bottom line for a product-driven strategy is: Best product wins!

One area of excellence is *product and process development.* Compared to U.S. cars, Japanese cars of the late 1950s (when cars from Japan came onto the market) were far inferior. But Japanese car manufacturers understood well that pursuing a product-driven strategy required product and process development. And they strove to improve the product—to make it better and better—to the extent that Japanese cars eventually surpassed the quality of U.S. cars.

For many years Fujitsu was satisfied with making copycat versions of IBM mainframes. Both had mediocre performances. In 1991, the company decided to stop matching IBM and to start making better computers than IBM. It's too early to tell, but this strategy is bound to produce better results.

A second area of excellence is *service.* IBM, which also pursues a product-driven strategy, is well aware of this requirement. Ask IBM clients what they admire most about IBM, and 99 out of 100 will say its service capability. IBM deliberately invests more resources in its service function than any other competitor and thus has a considerable edge in response time and infrequency of product failures.

In a product-driven mode, you maintain your competitive advantage by cultivating excellence in product development and service.

Market/User Class–Driven Strategy

An organization that is market/user class–driven must also cultivate excellence to optimize its strategy, but in dramatically different areas. A market/user-class–driven company has placed its destiny in the hands of a type of market or a class of users. Therefore, to survive and prosper, it must know its user class or market category better than any competitor. *Market* or *user research*, then, is one area of excellence. The company must know everything there is to know about its market or user in order to quickly detect any changes in habits, demographics, attitudes, or tastes. Procter & Gamble, which is consumer-driven, interviews consumers (particularly homemakers) over 2 million times per year in an attempt to anticipate trends that can be converted into product opportunities. Playboy does the same thing by monitoring changes in its subscribers through its magazine surveys each year.

A second area of excellence for a market/user class–driven company is *user loyalty.* Through a variety of means, these companies, over time, build customer loyalty to the company's products or brands. Then they trade on this loyalty. Over time, Johnson & Johnson has convinced its customers that its products are "safe." And it will not let anything infringe on the loyalty it has developed because of this guarantee. Whenever a Johnson & Johnson product might prove to be a hazard to a person's health, it is immediately removed from the market.

The Tylenol case in Chicago is a good example of how highly Johnson & Johnson values its users' loyalty. Even though "experts" predicted the death of Tylenol because they reasoned that Johnson & Johnson's recall was an admission of guilt, three months later Johnson & Johnson reintroduced the product, showed how the company had eliminated the possibility of tampering, demonstrated that the product was "safe" again, and traded on their users' loyalty to regain sales. Six months later Tylenol once more had the largest market share.

Production Capacity/Capability–Driven Strategy

When there is a glut of paper in the market, the first thing a paper company does is lower the price because the last thing they want to do is shut the mill. Therefore, to survive during the period of low prices, one has to have the lowest costs of any competitor. To achieve this, an area of excellence required is *manufacturing* or *plant efficiency*. This is why paper companies are forever investing their profits in their mills—to make them more and more efficient. An industry that has lost sight of this notion in the 1990s is the steel industry in the United States and central Europe. By not improving their plants, they lost business to the Italians and Japanese, who had done so. One notable exception in the United States is Allegheny Ludlum, which has done very well because it has the lowest costs of any steel mill, including the Japanese and Italian mills. As a result, Allegheny's revenues and profits have consistently improved. Its managers are unique in that they know the cost of each of perhaps 30,000 coils of steel floating around the company's seven plants, at any given stage of production. "The thing that scares me now is that we know our true costs, but competitors don't," says CEO Richard Simmons in a *Fortune* magazine article. "How can they make logical pricing decisions?"

Another industry, textiles, has lost a lot of ground to offshore competitors, but one exception stands out. Guilford Mills in Greensboro, North Carolina, is competing very successfully, and the reason is that its chief executive, Charles Hayes, knows that, as a production-capacity–driven organization, his company must excel at optimizing manufacturing efficiency. "We can make fabric as cheaply as anyone in the world," he says in an article in *Forbes* magazine. "We take that basic commodity, nylon lingerie fabric, and enhance it. The more we can do to it in the manufacturing process, the more we can sell it for and the higher our margins." In order to do this Hayes spends heavily on new equipment—over $36 million over 2 years—to gain the most automated knitting, dying, and fiber plants in the world.

A second area of excellence for the production capacity–driven strategy is *substitute marketing*. Capacity-driven companies excel at substituting what comes off their machines for other things. The paper people are trying to substitute paper for plastic; the plastic people are trying to substitute plastic for aluminum; concrete for steel. The same is true in the transportation industry where bus companies are trying to replace trains; train companies the airlines; and so forth.

Technology/Know-How–Driven Strategy

A company that is technology-driven uses technology as its edge. Thus, an area of excellence required to win under this strategy is *research*, either basic or applied. Sony, for example, spends 10 percent of its sales on research, which is 2 or 3 percent more than any competitor. Its motto, "research is the difference," is proof that the company's management recognizes the need to excel in this area.

By pushing the technology further than any competitor, new products and new markets will emerge. Technology-driven companies usually *create* markets rather than respond to needs and usually follow their technology wherever it leads them. Merck & Company is a good example of a company whose ex-CEO and chief strategist, Ray Vagelos, knew precisely what area of excellence must be fueled to deliver new products. Merck, at Vagelos's directive, poured hundreds of millions of dollars into research, as a technology-driven company should, and has come up with an ongoing stream of new products in an industry that introduces a new drug about as often as an aircraft manufacturer introduces a new airplane. It has consistently spent a greater share of its revenues on research than the rest of the industry. In 1986, the amount was $460 million, and it was increased to $1 billion in 1991, which was 11 percent of sales—more than any competitor. Its research teams *excel* and are on the leading edge of science in biochemistry, neurology, immunology, and molecular biology. Few other drug companies can match the breadth and depth of expertise Merck has in these areas.

Another CEO who has realized the importance of research as an area of excellence for his company is Edmund Pratt, Jr., of Pfizer Inc. From 1981 through 1990, he spent 8 percent of sales on R&D. In 1990 alone, the amount was $602 million, or 14 percent of revenues. Pfizer is in the process of launching nine new drugs which could have a potential of over $2 billion in sales for the company. "We've got new drugs coming out our ears," says a pleased Pratt.

His successor, William Steere, comes from the same mold and is perpetuating that investment. In 1994 the amount was $1 billion and the 1995 total will be $1.3 billion, which might surpass even Merck. As a result, the Pfizer new product hopper is brimming over.

Also in the pharmaceutical industry yet another CEO clearly understands the relationship between his company's driving force and its areas of excellence. This is Robert Bauman of Smith Kline Beecham in the United Kingdom. In an article appearing in the *Journal of Business Strategy*, Bauman articulated it in this manner: "The unifying theme of the company has always been a science based strategy [technology driving force]." As such, he allocated 80 percent of the firm's $800 million budget to six therapeutic areas of excellence. These are anti-infectives, biologicals, cardiovascular, central nervous system, gastrointestinal, and inflammation and tissue repair. Bauman expects that by 1996 the company will be generating 25 percent of its revenues from these strategic capabilities.

A second area of excellence for technology-driven companies is *applications marketing*. Technology-driven companies seem to have a knack for finding applications for their technology that call for highly differentiated products. For example, 3M used its coating technology to develop Post-it notepads and some 60,000 other products.

Sales/Marketing Method–Driven Strategy

The prosperity of a sales method–driven company depends on the reach and effectiveness of its selling method. As a result, the first area of excellence companies such as Avon and Mary Kay must cultivate is the ongoing *recruitment* of door-to-door salespeople. Mary Kay has had tremendous success in the last few years because it has been able to draw several hundred thousand women to sell its product. Avon's fortunes have suffered because its sales force has dropped considerably during that same period.

The second area of excellence needed to succeed with this strategy is improving the *effectiveness* of the selling method. Door-to-door companies are constantly training their salespeople in product knowledge, product demonstration, and selling skills. Growth and profits come from improving volume through the diversity and effectiveness of its sales methods.

Distribution Method–Driven Strategy

To win the war while pursuing distribution method–driven strategy, you must first have the *most effective* distribution method. As a result, you must offer products and services that use or enhance your distribution system. Second, you must always look for ways to optimize the *effectiveness*, either in cost or value, of that system. That is your edge. You should also look for any form of distribution that could bypass or make your distribution method obsolete.

Both Federal Express and Wal-Mart are good examples of distribution method–driven companies. They are constantly striving to improve the efficiency of their respective distribution systems—the heartbeat of their business. David Glass, CEO of Wal-Mart, has stated, "Our distribution facilities are one of the keys to our success. If we do anything better than other folks, that's it."

Knowing that, Glass spent $500 million in the last five years on a computer system that links the company to its suppliers in order to lower costs even further.

Fred Smith, CEO of Federal Express, also knows what the strategic heartbeat of his business is when he says, "The main difference between us and our competitors is that we have more capacity to track, trace and control items in the system." To demonstrate his adherence to this principle, FedEx recently introduced a new service—software that allows customers to track parcels from their own PCs.

Natural Resource–Driven Strategy

Successful resource-driven companies excel at doing just that—*exploring* and finding the type of resources they are engaged in. Exxon considers itself to be the best at "exploring for oil and gas," and it does this better than any competitor. It was the recognition of this fact that led Exxon to drop its office equipment division. There's not much oil and gas to be found there; plus, that kind of venture requires excellence in areas Exxon does not possess.

John Bookout, ex-CEO of Shell USA, is a good example of a strategist who understands his company's areas of excellence. Shell's particular expertise is "enhanced oil recovery in offshore waters deeper than 600 feet." In this area, Shell has few rivals, as he explained to *Forbes* magazine. In 1983, Shell drilled a project called Bullwinkle in the Gulf of Mexico at a depth of 1350 feet. Outsiders thought the project was too risky, particularly since Shell did not spread the risk by taking other partners in on the deal. "You can't believe how easy that decision was," he says. "It took us 30 minutes in the boardroom." The reason? Bookout was banking on Shell's area of excellence in deepwater recovery.

Size/Growth– or Return/Profit–Driven Strategy

Companies that choose either a size/growth–driven or a return/profit–driven strategy require excellence in financial management. One such area is *portfolio management*. This means proficiency at moving assets around in order to maximize the size/growth or return/profit of the entire organization.

A second area of excellence is *information systems*. These companies usually have a corporate "big brother" group that constantly monitors the performance of its various divisions, and, as soon as a problem is detected, an attempt to correct or expunge it is made. Harold Geneen had such a group at ITT.

Importance of Areas of Excellence

Why are areas of excellence an integral part of new product innovation? No company has the resources to develop skills equally in all areas. Therefore, another strategic decision that management must wrestle with, once the driving force has been identified, is to clearly identify those two or three skills that are critical and to give those areas *preferential* resources. In good times, these areas receive additional resources; in bad times they are the last areas you cut. For example, 3M, which is a technology-driven company, had a chairman—Alan Jacobsen—who clearly recognized this concept. When Jacobsen took over as chief executive, he set about to improve 3M's profitability. He asked all his division heads to cut expenses by as much as 35 percent, but he spared R&D expenditures. In fact, he *increased* R&D from 4.5 percent of sales to 6.6 percent. The reason: Research is a required area of excellence for a technology-driven company. Ever since then 3M has been on a roll spitting out 300 to 400 new products each year, and its stock has more than doubled in the last five years. "Des" Desimone, 3M's current CEO, also understands this concept: In an attempt to rev up 3M's product creation pace, he has increased R&D's percentage another point.

Another company that clearly understands its strategic capabilities and is leveraging these as this book is being written is Johnson & Johnson, the author's former employer. In the same week, the company announced that it was acquiring Nutrigena as well as the clinical diagnostic division of Kodak. Why these two seemingly unrelated businesses. Simply because both companies' products are aimed at the same class of users that J&J's other businesses target—*doctors, nurses, patients*, and *mothers*. As a result, J&J management feels confident that since these new products "fit" the *heartbeat*, its strategic capabilities will also be leveraged into these new businesses to make them even more successful.

A company, therefore, has two key decisions to make if it wishes to have a successful product innovation program. First, it must determine which strategic area will *drive* the business and thus the direction of the organization. Second, it must decide what *areas of excellence* or *capabilities* it must cultivate to keep its strategy healthy (see Figures 7-9 and 7-10). These areas of excellence should receive preferential treatment—fueled with more resources in order to develop a level of proficiency greater than any competitor and then *leveraged across the broadest array* of products, customers, and markets. Once resources are diverted elsewhere, proficiency diminishes, and the company loses its product innovation edge vis-à-vis its competitors.

AREAS OF EXCELLENCE

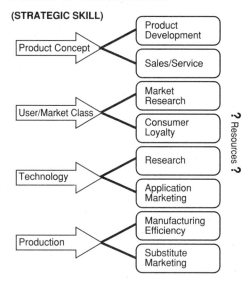

Figure 7-9.

AREAS OF EXCELLENCE

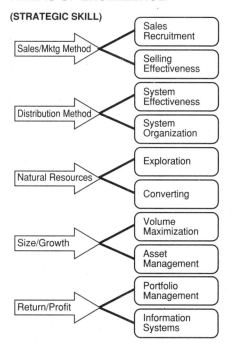

Figure 7-10.

8

Create Products
for the Future,
Not the Present

During our research for this book over the years, we attempted to understand why many companies seem to concentrate their entire product creation effort on incremental or marginal improvements to existing products. This type of product innovation is a necessary part of business, but it leads only to *marginal* increases in revenue. The cause of such marginal results, in our humble view, is too much focus on the customer. In view of the great number of consultants that earn their living promoting the concept that firms today must get closer to their customers—be customer-driven as they call it—the fact remains that very few *new* product concepts come from customers. If the focus of a new product creation program is restricted to the analysis of customer needs, the company will more than likely end up with product extensions and not new-to-the-market product concepts.

The reason is simple. Customers are usually good at identifying performance gaps in products they are currently using, but they are not very skillful at identifying future trends and converting these into future needs. Most truly new-to-the-market products were conceived in the mind of the maker of the product, not the consumer of that product. The list of examples is limitless. No customer ever asked Thomas Edison to develop a light bulb. No customer ever asked Spencer Fry to develop a Post-it Note. No customer ever asked Akio Morita to develop a Walkman. No customer ever asked Steve Jobs and

Steve Wozniak to develop a personal computer. No customer asked Lee Iacocca to develop the Mustang. No customer ever asked Craig McCaw to develop a cellular telephone network. No customer ever asked Ted Turner to develop an international, all-news television network. No customer ever asked Hal Sperlich to develop a minivan. No customer ever asked Ray Kroc to build a chain of stores to sell hamburgers. No customer ever asked Wayne Huezinga to build a chain of retail outlets to rent videos. No customer ever asked Bill Gates to develop Windows software. The list is limitless!

The reason that new-to-the-market concepts do not originate in the minds of customers is very simple. Customers can convert performance gaps in current products into explicit needs, but these gaps are rarely the source of needs that gives birth to new-to-the-market product concepts. New-to-the-market product concepts come from the identification of *implicit* needs that stem from the interpretation of *future* trends. Furthermore, implicit needs are the result of two elements:

- Anticipation of future trends that identify implicit, future needs

- Understanding of strategic capabilities that can be leveraged to create concepts for new-to-the-market products

View of the Future Business Arena

The key to the creation of concepts for new-to-the-market products is the ability to envision what the future business arena that will face the company in the *future* will look like. In other words, it is the ability to look into the future and anticipate what trends or events will shape the "look" of the arena that the corporation plays in. The second skill is then the ability to match the strategic capabilities of the corporation with new-to-the-market products and exploit these before the competition does.

The following is a checklist of areas which are usually dynamic in nature and where one can constantly find trends and/or events that can give rise to new implicit needs:

- Economic environment
- Political environment
- Regulatory and legislative environment
- Demographic and social environment
- Market conditions

- Customer/user profiles and habits
- Competitive environment
- Technology evolution
- Product content and features
- Manufacturing processes and capabilities
- Sales/marketing methods
- Delivery/distribution methods and/or systems
- Human, financial, natural resources

To identify new, implicit needs, the technique is quite simple. Place yourself in a time machine and project yourself x number of years into the future and describe what each of these elements will "look" like then. Such a scenario is bound to give birth to an unlimited number of new product opportunities. Following are examples of people or firms that have done exactly that.

Economic Environment

Why are so many companies currently scrambling to establish themselves in China? The reason is simple. China's economy is projected to be the fastest growing one in the world for the next 10 or 15 years. That trend will make China the second biggest industrial country on this planet by the year 2020. Recognizing what China is today and envisioning what it might be tomorrow will offer enterprising companies like Caterpillar a multitude of new needs that will undoubtedly give birth to as many new product concepts. These new, implicit needs might also give birth to new products that could then be resold in Caterpillar's existing markets.

Regulatory and Legislative Trends

One individual is currently positioned to become the most important manufacturer of cheese in Europe, and he will achieve that from the United States. That person's name is Fermo Jaeckle, who foresaw, back in 1988, that Europe could not continue to support its generous farm subsidies and would have to change its regulations."It had already become clear to me," he recently told *Forbes* magazine, "that agricultural policies would eventually bankrupt the European Community."

What did Jaeckle do once he recognized this trend as well as a second one which was the lowering value of the U.S. dollar? He went out and purchased an old cheese facility, not in Europe, but in Monroe, Wisconsin. Not to make its traditional American cheese—Muenster—but to convert it to making the best of European-type cheeses such as gruyere, havarti, fontinas, butter kase, and raclette. With the advent of the recent GATT agreement which will reduce and eventually eliminate these European subsidies, Jaeckle is now the only United States–based company prepared to offer European-type cheeses with a 20 to 75 cents per pound cost advantage. And the Europeans will never know their favorite cheese comes from the United States!

Demographic and Social Trends

As mentioned in a previous chapter, one of the important demographic trends now in progress in most Western countries is the aging of the population—in other words, the trend that will produce a population that will have 50 percent of its total number over age 55 by the year 2010.

One individual who has noticed this trend and decided to capitalize on it is Rick Adler, who has founded a new type of marketing company (called The Senior Network) totally dedicated to this market segment. Rick's company offers a wide range of services, all geared to this market, such as market research, statistics, advertising, promotion, merchandising, and samplings. These services are naturally sold to other companies trying to reach this market, such as insurance companies, food companies, and airline companies. The company even publishes its own magazine with a circulation of 3.7 million individuals in this market segment and distributed through leisure centers where seniors congregate. Naturally, advertising space in the magazine is resold to client organizations.

Another organization that anticipated this same demographic trend and is set to capitalize on it is a company called Elderhostel. Tapping into the fond memories that many of the over-55 population have of the youth hostels they stayed in while they traveled Europe as students on shoestring budgets, this company is developing a chain of hostels for that segment. This hostel will offer slightly better, but yet cheaper, rooms, together with a program of "intellectual" activities tailored to a more sophisticated group of people.

Another demographic change that was recently noticed by one of our clients in Europe is the growing influx of people who live in the suburbs but who travel to the city to work. This daily influx has creat-

Figure 8-1. Bombardier Eurorail's combination bus and tramcar.

ed transportation nightmares for both the cities—pollution—and the individual traveler who has to connect among two or more modes of transport to get to work. Bombardier Eurorail saw this change as an opportunity to create a unique new product—a combination bus and tramcar. The product (Figure 8-1) is a bus with normal rubber tires and a steel wheel up front that can be lifted or lowered on demand. The concept is simple. In the city, it is a tram with the steel front wheel down and following a single (instead of the traditional dual-track system) track imbedded in the road. Once it leaves the city limits, the steel wheel is lifted and the tram becomes a bus, free to navigate where it wants. No more connections for the passenger. The first of these unique new vehicles has been ordered by the city of Caen, in France, and will be operational in 1995.

Yet another company that has detected a societal trend that has given birth to a new-to-the-market product is the French company J. C. Decaux. J. C. Decaux is in the outdoor advertising business. In France, it has found an ingenious way of getting advertising messages to the masses. The company conceived the concept of small bus shelters which it provides to communities all over France in return for the community's permission to allow Decaux to sell advertising space on the side panels. Now it is bringing a slightly different concept to the United States based on a need that has emerged as a result of a growing social trend in the country's cities. That trend, noticed by Decaux, is the growing number of people such as taxi drivers, pregnant mothers, police officers, and the homeless who periodically need access to

Figure 8-2. J. C. Decaux's high-tech combination washroom toilet.

sanitary services. The concept: a new, high-tech combination wash-room toilet that is also crime intolerant (see Figure 8-2).

Customer/User Profile and Habits

The best example of a trend that gave birth to a very successful new-to-the-market product was Akio Morita's detection of the increasing number of people jogging back in the 1970s. Because of his love for classical music, Morita anticipated that many people would love to have their music "portable" and thus the creation of the Walkman. Mr. Morita also anticipated another implicit need—that many people would like to see TV movies several times—and thus the birth of still another very successful new-to-the-market product, the VCR!

Bill Gates, founder of Microsoft, has noticed the increasing number of people who travel and also visit museums. Why not bring the museum into the home? And that is exactly one of the projects that his firm is working on. Software that will contain a database of the paintings of the world's greatest artists that can be viewed in the home, at a moment's notice on a wall-to-wall screen (because Gates also foresees this trend happening as well).

Competitive Environment

One of the key trends that occurred in the United States as a result of the deregulation of the airline industry in the 1980s was the advent of regional or "niche" carriers. While the larger airlines tried to capitalize on this event by merging and consolidating themselves into larger and larger airlines, some people capitalized on the same trend by doing the exact opposite. They started small, more nimble airlines to exploit all the destinations that the larger, consolidated carriers were giving up. Thus the birth of Southwest and People's Express. The trend continues to this day with the recent entry of Valujet and Kiwi Airlines. Someone should be on the lookout in Europe as the same trend is starting to develop there. As the major carriers start dialogues to merge their operations, that trend is bound to produce opportunities to any astute innovator.

Technology Evolution

Emerging trends in the technology area always provide ample opportunities for new product creation. Bob O'Brien, CEO of NEXTEL, is such an individual. O'Brien has seen opportunity where others have not. With the increasing trend in the use of cellular telephones, he noted that another technology, that of radio to dispatch taxis, could be used to transmit data and voice. For the last few years, O'Brien has been furiously buying out as many radio dispatch companies across the United States as he has been able to identify. To date, he has assembled a network that covers 80 percent of the U.S. population, and he is now ready to offer an alternative to the cellular phone companies.

Ted Turner is another individual who foresaw a technological trend that led to the creation of CNN. That trend was the convergence of cable and satellite technologies. Unlike the traditional networks such as ABC, CBS, and NBC, which had locked themselves into a standard broadcast technology, Turner anticipated that the convergence of these two technologies would provide the opportunity to make the dissemination of news a worldwide opportunity. The other trend that Turner read very well was that of vanishing borders and the growth of English as a worldwide "business" language. I am certain that, like me, many of you have been surprised by the number of people who are interviewed on CNN from around the world who speak impeccable English—even the students who appeared on CNN during the Tienanmen Square uprisings of 1989.

Manufacturing Processes and Capabilities

I mentioned in an earlier chapter the success that an upstart bicycle company from Connecticut called Cannondale Corp. was having with bicycles tailored to individual's needs. Another company has noticed another trend and has given birth to a new-to-the-market bicycle product. That company is Montague Corp. in Cambridge, Massachusetts, which just introduced a "folding" bicycle (Figure 8-3). Why a folding bicycle? Simply because the owners of the company had noticed two emerging trends. The first was an increasing number of people who like to bicycle and travel but who do not have storage space in either their apartments or in the trunk of their cars. Then there are the people who travel to their biking destinations by airplane. The second trend detected was the new generation of lightweight materials and high-

Figure 8-3. Montague Corporation's folding bicycle.

tech composites. The company has introduced a wide array of bicycles to satisfy the needs of any person from the casual rider to that of the more experienced, mountain trail expert.

Sales/Marketing Methods

Probably the best example of the creation of not only a new-to-the-market service but of an entire industry is the Home Shopping Network. Noticing the trend toward less and less time to shop through the traditional, away-from-home methods such as supermarkets and department stores, the detectors of this trend conceived a new service that allows people to shop at home through their television sets. The advent of PCs and Internet will accelerate this trend.

Conclusion

These are but a few of the numerous products that have been created by someone's ability to read what the business arena would look like in the years ahead and respond with concepts for new-to-the-market products.

The advantage of this approach is threefold:

- It provides the conceptor to introduce *differentiated* products.
- It allows the conceptor to build in *barriers to entry* such as patents.
- It provides a period of *exclusivity* that brings *premium* prices.

In four or five short statements, describe what your business arena will look like in *x* years down the road, *with or without* your company's participation, using these questions as a guide.

Process Questions

- What will the *economic environment* look like in *x* years?
- What will the *political environment* look like in *x* years?
- What will the *regulatory and legislative environment* look like in *x* years?
- What will the *demographic and social environment* look like in *x* years?
- What will the *markets* look like in *x* years?
- What will *customer/user profiles* and *habits* look like in *x* years?
- What will the *competitive environment* look like in *x* years?

- What will the next two or three *generations of technology* look like in x years?

- What *features and content* will *products* have in the next x years?

- What will *manufacturing processes and capabilities* look like in x years?

- What will *sales/marketing methods* look like in x years?

- What will *delivery/distribution* methods and systems look like in x years?

- What will *human, financial, and natural* resources look like in x years?

As Peter Drucker said: "The best way to manage the future? *Create it!*"

9

The Future of Successful New Product Innovation: Market Fragmentation

In our work with the CEOs and management teams of over 300 corporations worldwide, we are constantly being told by these executives that change, particularly technological change, is happening faster and faster. As a result, they claim, no one can keep up—much less predict anything—with the avalanche of changes facing a business today.

The Myth of Rapid Technological Change

Although a part of the above observation is sometimes true, the idea that technological change happens too quickly to be anticipated is somewhat of a myth. Our own work would offer a different hypothesis. Our view is that most executives get caught by surprise because they have not been looking! And when you have not been looking, every change catches you by surprise!

The fact is that technological change takes 20 to 30 years to find a commercially viable application and then another 50 to 70 years before it has an impact on all the nooks and crannies that it eventually will affect. However, if you have not been looking, even a change that is only creeping along will seem to hit you very fast. Two examples come to mind. The first is the invention of electricity. Although invented in the 1860s, it only found a few successful applications in the 1870s and 1880s. Most of the applications of electricity which are now taken as a given were not developed for another two to three decades later. The same is true of robotics, lasers, and fiber optics—all technologies invented in the 1950s but barely finding commercially viable applications today—some 40 years later. The microprocessor is yet another example. Although invented in the 1960s, and although it gave birth to the personal computer in the 1970s, the fact is that in spite of the billions of dollars invested in these products by corporations all over the world, the products have had no effect on the productivity of these companies so far. Only now, in 1995, are we starting to see the potential impact that these machines might have. And we have only seen a very small percentage of the potential applications of the microprocessor.

Although corporate executives would claim that they are constantly bombarded by changes that affect their business, in reality there are very few *macro* changes that have significant impact on corporations. Failure to recognize these macro trends can mean corporate death. However, the company that does detect a macro change early in its evolution and constructs a strategy to capitalize on it can reap substantial reward.

The Impact of Unnoticed Macro Changes

There are some changes, macro in nature, that affect every product made by every company on the planet. Frequently, unfortunately, many executives completely fail to notice these until it is too late.

It is a fact, today, that 50 percent of the population of the United States, Japan, and most European countries will be 55 years and over by the year 2010. No one can change that. And that change will have an effect on every product made by every company in the world.

For example, Caterpillar had better be thinking today, of designing its large machines in a manner to be operated by frail old men or women. Why? Simply because there will not be enough big, young men with big biceps to move all those levers. Another example came out of our work with Texaco. When a group of their executives used the process described in this book, they started questioning the concept of the self-service gas station. They started asking themselves if the notion of asking people to get out of their cars to serve themselves might still be viable when people are older and less mobile. Therefore, why not have a small robot next to each pump that takes a customer's credit card, processes it, puts the nozzle in the gas tank, activates it and then hands you back the card. All accomplished without the customer leaving the driver's seat.

Macro Changes

Two such macro trends are currently at work today. One is a demographic change—the aging population of most Western countries—which will affect every company in the world for the next 25 years. The other has already occurred but has been missed by most corporate, particularly in the United States. The most significant change of the last 15 years is that the majority of the economies of the Western world have gone from "push" economies to "pull" economies. "What's the difference?" you may ask. "Very substantial," I would answer.

Push to Pull Economy

In a *push economy* there is more demand than supply, and the *producer* reigns. From 1945 to the mid-1970s such was the case in the West. Most companies, particularly U.S. ones, were riding this wave. Everything they produced was immediately gobbled up by long lines of customers craving their products. One only needs to go back to the introduction of television in the mid-1950s to understand this phenomenon. If you were around back then, you will remember how the entire neighborhood would gather at the window of the local appliance store to watch the TV set through the store window. The next morning, there was always a long line of customers waiting to purchase their first TV. It didn't matter much to the customer that resolution was poor and that the picture kept rotating on the screen; the goal was to get a set before the store sold out—more demand than supply. This situation lasted until the mid-1970s.

Today, the opposite situation exists. With the advent of Japanese, Korean, Singaporean, Taiwanese, and European products, there is more supply than demand. As a result, the rules of the game have changed significantly. In a *pull economy*, the *customer* reigns. Unfortunately, few CEOs have noticed. (See Figure 9-1.)

Market Fragmentation versus Segmentation

How does one deal with a push versus a pull economy? In a push economy, the producer controls the market and the key to success is market segmentation. This is the concept of grouping large numbers of customers with *similar* needs together and providing them with a generic

ECONOMY

PUSH	PULL
⬆ **DEMAND VS. SUPPLY**	⬆ **SUPPLY VS. DEMAND**
PRODUCER	**CUSTOMER**
MARKET SEGMENTATION	**MARKET FRAGMENTATION**
LARGE # CUSTOMERS SIMILAR NEEDS	**SMALLER # CUSTOMERS DISSIMILAR NEEDS**
GENERIC PRODUCT	**TAILORED PRODUCT**
COMMODITY PRICES	**PREMIUM PRICES**
LONG PRODUCTION RUNS	**SHORTER PRODUCTION RUNS**
EFFICIENT MANUFACTURING	**FLEXIBILE, EFFECTIVE MANUFACTURING**
LONG PRODUCT CYCLES	**SHORTER PRODUCT CYCLES**
STRONG BRAND LOYALTY	**LITTLE BRAND LOYALTY**
PRODUCT INNOVATION	**PROCESS INNOVATION**
FIXED RULES	**CHANGING RULES**
STURDY AND STABLE	**FAST AND NIMBLE**

Figure 9-1. (*Copyright by Decision Processes International. All rights reserved.*)

product. It's the Henry Ford approach to business. "You can have any color car you want as long as it's black." This has been the approach followed by all U.S. producers since the end of World War II. But unfortunately, it does not work in a pull economy. A company must practice the opposite concept of *market fragmentation* to be successful.

The opposite concept of market fragmentation means identifying smaller groups of customers with *dissimilar* needs and responding with *customized* products. The world's most successful companies today are practicing market fragmentation. Companies in trouble are still clinging to the outdated market segmentation. Again, a variety of examples exist.

In the automobile industry, which was probably the first to go from push to pull, one of the most successful companies is Toyota. The reason is simple. Toyota has so mastered its business and manufacturing processes that a customer can enter a dealer's office in Japan on Monday morning, configure the car he or she wants, and take delivery of it on Friday afternoon—custom-made to the buyer's specifications.

Even BMW, the German automaker, attributes its current success to market fragmentation. As *Business Week* reported in a 1991 article entitled "'Grill to Grill' with Japan":

> In Europe, where BMW gets 75% of its sales, most cars are made to order. That's why BMW offers a big à la carte menu of models, engines, colors, and options. "Each customer can have a unique car," says Eberhard von Kuenheim (CEO). Japanese competitors offer far fewer choices. He complains: "They are building 100, 200, even 400 exactly identical cars a day."

I hate to think what he would say about the U.S. manufacturers.

Sony markets a different version of its Walkman in Norway than it does in Sweden, two of its smallest worldwide markets. Why? Sony discovered that these two areas had unique needs that required a slightly different product.

Twenty months after 3M introduced its unique Post-it Notes, the company had developed more than 100 versions of the original product to cater to a variety of slightly different needs in the marketplace. No other competitor was able to keep up with such a pace of product proliferation.

Castrol, the oil lubricant specialist, has no oil reserves nor does it own any refineries or service stations. What Castrol does have, however, is over 3000 different formulas of lubricants, each tailored to a specific application. While the major oil companies try to satisfy the market with one or two generic lubricants, Castrol can provide a specific formula especially conceived to fulfill the requirements of each customer's specific application.

FLEXcon, a client based in Spencer, Massachusetts, has a similar approach. Whereas the giant chemical companies provide multipurpose, generic adhesives to printers who produce printed packaging material, FLEXcon develops a special formula for each printer. FLEXcon's ability to tailor a solution to meet each printer's specific need represents that companies competitive advantage.

In the retailing business, Sears is suffering from a double whammy. On one hand, a number of specialty retailers are fragmenting the market away from Sears. Sears's strategy of being all things to all people—as reflected by the broad array of merchandise, from furniture to financial services—is being decimated by a new brand of retailers such as The Limited and The Gap, each catering to a much narrower range of needs. On the other hand, a couple of players such as Wal-Mart and Home Depot are changing the rules of play. Don't buy shares in Sears for a number of years to come.

Even McDonald's is feeling the pinch of market fragmentation. A host of smaller, more nimble competitors are forcing McDonald's to rethink its entire strategy. Companies such as Chili's, Taco Bell, Olive Garden, and others are dividing and conquering what was once a large, homogeneous market for hamburgers.

In the mundane world of pens, pencils, and markers, the Sanford Company of Illinois produces a return on equity of 24 percent and sales increases of 14 percent per year. How? By fragmenting the market to pieces. Sanford keeps broadening the market by niching it to death. Sanford has markers for all types of applications, from marking clothes in laundromats to nonsmearing markers for use on fax paper. In between, it has watercolor markers for toddlers of every age and talent. Again, the myth of the mature market has been proven to be false. As *Forbes* observed in the August 5, 1991, issue about this company: "As the fountain pen was dying 40 years ago, few would have thought Sanford would survive into the 1990s. Fewer still would have predicted that the market would price it like a growth stock. Impressive job, Hank Pearsall."

In the beer industry most brewers are having a difficult time growing tire businesses and maintaining their margins. The reason? A group of entrepreneurs, evolving as micro-brewmeisters, are fragmenting the large brewers' markets to smithereens with a host of regional brands that many times sell only in their respective cities. It is reported that over 500 such regional brands have sprung up in the last five years. The national brewers, caught off guard by this phenomenon, should have anticipated it, since the same has occurred in Germany and Britain, where there is a brewery in every village, let alone every city.

Belgium may host the ultimate in terms of market fragmentors. In one of the smallest countries in Europe (population 10 million), there are between 500 and 800 breweries. In Belgium, one finds market fragmentors that are fragmenting market fragments! One can find raspberry beer, wheat beer, red beer, golden beer, 12% alcohol beer, grape beer, beer made in abbeys, beer with spices, and even "dark" beer for

Christmas. The concept of market fragmentation is strong and healthy in Belgium!

Even mighty American Express has discovered the concept of market fragmentation. After decades of offering only two versions of its cards, green and gold, the company has just announced that in the next 18 months it will scrap this approach and will introduce 13 new versions, each aimed at a fragment of these two initial segments.

The most successful manufacturer of home appliances in Europe, Electrolux, has also learned that market fragmentation works. Electrolux has recognized that Northern Europeans want large refrigerators since they shop only once a week, whereas the French want small ones since most shop each day. Northerners want their freezers on the bottom while southerners like their freezers on top. And Electrolux has responded with a wide array of tailored products to satisfy all these needs. Whirlpool, on the other hand—relatively new to Europe—has taken the opposite track. It is trying to sell a standard product across Europe. Time will tell if this strategy will succeed.

Differentiated versus Commodity Products

One of the first impacts of market fragmentation is that it almost makes commodity products and their providers obsolete. Because the practitioners of market segmentation respond with generic products that attempt to satisfy large groups of users, these products are usually easily duplicatable and, before long, become "commodity" items. Market fragmentation, however, results in a wide variety of custom-made products, each differentiated to satisfy a unique set of requirements. Because customer needs are always evolving, so too are the products. This makes it more difficult for competitors to emulate.

In fact, the companies and industries that are struggling today are the ones that have not adjusted to market fragmentation and are losing ground to those that are practicing this concept. The strategy of the "fragmentor" is to identify large, commodity markets and to fragment them into smaller pieces to the fragmentor's advantage.

In the media industry, CBS, ABC, and NBC are going through this trauma. The industry is being fragmented by the cable providers who, in turn, are fragmenting programming to address the more specific needs of smaller segments of the audience. Thus, the remarkable growth and success of MTV, A&E, ESPN, and others.

Ted Turner is running ahead of the pack. Not only has he changed the rules of play with his worldwide news network CNN, but he is also practicing market fragmentation through cable television. In addition to his news network, Turner has introduced an all-movie channel for movie buffs, an all-sports network for sports buffs, and—an all-cartoon network for cartoon buffs.

Bill Ziff of Ziff Communications and Dale Lang of Lang Communications did the same thing to the barons of the print media. For several decades the goal of magazine publishers was to publish a magazine that could find an audience of 7 to 10 million readers. Several did at one time and became known as the "seven sisters." These included *McCall's, Redbook,* and *Good Housekeeping.* Lang and Ziff have done exactly the opposite. Lang is the publisher of a number of women's magazines, each tailored to a unique set of feminine needs. One, for example, is called *Working Woman* and another is called *Working Mother.* Each has a subscriber base of only a million readers, but the magazines are highly successful. In fact, *Working Woman* has been the most successful of any magazine launched in the last decade.

Ziff, on the other hand, can be considered the founder of "special interest" magazines. He started such titles as *Car and Driver, Yachting, PC Magazine, MacUser,* and *Computer Shopper.* Ziff clearly detected the shift from market segmentation, as being practiced by the seven sisters, to market fragmentation. As he told *Forbes* in an interview in the June 10, 1991, issue: "When I started in this business, mass magazines were dominant. Today we live in an age of stratified, separated, targeted markets that are information-hungry. The future of all advertising-supported media is *narrow casting,* not broadcasting."

Hallmark once dominated the market for greeting cards, Today, 70 percent of the market has been fragmented by a dozen or so smaller companies that offer a card for just about any occasion, including no occasion.

In the 1970s, Adolph Coors, the brewing company, was in dire straits. Its growth had stopped and so had its profits. In the 1980s, Coors discovered market fragmentation. When the "light" beer craze arrived, both Miller and Anheuser-Busch introduced one brand and tried to capture the largest share of the market. Coors, on the other hand, introduced three different brands, each tailored to a different set of customers. One in particular called the Silver Bullet was geared especially to women. As a result, Coors doubled its sales in the 1980s and has edged its way up to third place next to Busch and Miller. Coors' objective is to displace Miller in second place by the end of this decade by more fragmentation.

Premium Price versus Low Price

One of the disadvantages of the market segmentation approach is that it leads to generic products, as already mentioned, and to generic prices. Because all products are very similar, so are the prices. And most transactions have a tendency to drift to the level of "low price wins," because customers see no difference in one product compared to another.

The advantage of market fragmentation is often the opposite. Products have been tailored to very specific needs, so the "solution" is usually different from the generic product, and added value can be perceived by each customer. This allows for *premium* pricing, and each transaction is concluded on the basis of value instead of price. Higher margins are therefore possible.

Both Lang and Ziff got premium prices for their publications compared to the publishers of the seven sisters. The reason is simple. Their magazines deliver to a narrower but more targeted audience with differentiated needs. The same is true at FLEXcon.

Another example of market fragmentation that brings premium prices is a small but growing company called Message! Check Corp. Located in Seattle and started by Priscilla Beard, this company makes personalized checks for groups or organizations who wish to personalize the graphics and the message on the blank check. It prints checks which carry messages from Greenpeace, Mothers Against Drunk Drivers, Vietnam Veterans of America, and a host of others. All these sell for twice what the traditional check printers charge, and Beard can't keep up with demand.

In yet another industry where fragmentation is fast taking over, premium prices are being realized. This is the cable industry where different channels are being programmed more and more by specialty broadcasters catering to smaller and smaller audiences but bringing higher and higher prices. There is, for example, a channel called the Military Channel which reaches 3 million subscribers on military bases in the United States. Whereas CNN obtains $4.50 per thousand viewers for a 30-second spot, the Military Channel gets $7.50, an 80 percent premium.

A company called Quidel Corp. has devised the ultimate use of market fragmentation to justify premium prices. Quidel markets pregnancy test kits. One brand called Conceive is found in one part of a drug store and retails for $9.99. Another brand called RapidVue is found is another part of the drug store and retails for $6.99. The product inside each box is exactly the same. What's different? The packaging. The

Conceive product has pink packaging with a smiling infant. The RapidVue one is in a plain wrapping with no picture. Why the difference? "The market definitely divides between the women who want babies and those who don't." says CEO Steven Frankel. He explains the difference in price: "People buy hope. In your case, they pay more for hope than for possible relief."

In the sunglass industry, two companies—Ray-Ban and Nikon—are trying to out-fragment each other—and both at premium prices. Ray-Ban has taken the track of offering over 80 different frame styles. Nikon, on other hand, offers a wide variety of lens, each tailored to a slightly different use. There is the Nikon CE lens for skiers that allows a low percentage (6 percent) of light through. For divers, there's the Nikon LE lens which allows up to 22 percent of the light through. Then there are lens for hiking, flying, shooting, and waterskiing—all at prices several notches higher than ordinary glasses. Nikon and Ray-Ban have both recognized that people's perception of a product can be changed and higher prices can be had.

In the telecommunication service industry these exists a company called Mtel. Mtel sells paging services, a service generally seen by all of Mtel's competitors as a commodity, undifferentiated service where lowest price wins. John Palmer, Mtel's CEO, doesn't agree, however, and he is proving the commodity view wrong. Under the Skytel name, the company offers basic nationwide paging services. Starting next July, however, the company will introduce a new two-way wireless communication network aimed at travelers who not only need to be contacted but also may have to respond. This new service, called Destineer, will be priced at a premium. The company sees all kinds of other customer fragments with special needs that could also be served through differentiated services at premium prices.

Even in the mundane world of rubber tires one man has also come to this conclusion. That person is Stanley Gault who took over as Goodyear's CEO in 1991. Although told time after time that "a tire was a tire was a tire" and that nothing more could be done to improve the product, Gault refused to accept this conclusion and insisted that some brainpower be applied to rethink the tire. Presto!—the Aquatred was born. A tire with a furrow down the middle to repel water and provide better traction sells at premium prices and now accounts for 8.5 percent of the company's profits. Since its introduction, Goodyear has introduced 22 new tires in a two-year period for 4-wheel all-terrain vehicles, vans, minivans, and pick-up trucks. The fragmentation fo the tire industry is bound to continue. Another one of our clients, Steelcord (a division of Bekaert in Belgium), recently received a request to provide the steelcord to make tires for a new Honda sports car which will have four different tires—one for each wheel! Goodyear will probably be the manufacturer. In fact, the tire industry is an excellent example of one that is experiencing all phases of the switch from market segmentation to market fragmentation. The sequence went something like this:

- A tire for all cars
- A tire for each size of car
- A tire for each model of car
- A tire for each wheel

Short Runs versus Long Runs

A great advantage of market segmentation is that it provides the producer with long manufacturing runs that enable it to attain maximum production efficiencies and, thus, profits. Unfortunately, the opposite is again the case in market fragmentation. Manufacturing versatility, not efficiency, is the key skill in this new mode. Again, U.S. companies have been slow to notice this change. As Michael Dertouzos, director of MIT's Laboratory for Computer Science, has pointed out in an article in an issue of *Chief Executive:*

> U.S. industry clings to outmoded strategies, like inflexible mass production of a large number of standard goods that does not reflect the growing demand for individualized custom quality products. This system, pioneered by Henry Ford, can be likened to a gigantic wheel of production, where workers, suppliers, and other participants are highly specialized cogs. The objective is to keep the wheel turning, no matter what. Anyone who misbehaves is replaced. By contrast, the new systems of production, both in the best-practice U.S. companies and abroad, entail a nimbler approach where broadly trained workers produce shorter runs of tailored goods. They are winning over the older system of mass production.

An industry currently undergoing the trials and tribulations of the transition from a push to pull mode is that of textiles. In the United States, textile manufacturers have concentrated on materials that can be produced in large quantities such as denim and sheeting. The problem they face, however, is that the retailers that are winning today are those that are fragmenting the market with a host of styles and fashions that require a much wider variety of materials and finishes but in smaller quantities. These are retailers such as The Limited and The

Gap. Both these companies are going offshore to satisfy their requirements, not because these manufacturers are less costly but because they are more flexible. As Lesly Wexler, CEO of The Limited, told *Business Week:* "The problem with U.S. textile mills is that they don't make what we want to buy." In a pull economy, the customer is king!

Production Efficiency versus Production Versatility

Under a system that stresses long production runs and commodity products that can easily be duplicated by competitors, the key to winning is to become the low-cost producer. The concept of market fragmentation, however, focuses on production versatility. In other words, versatility is the ability to change from one product to another on the same line without losing efficiency.

In Germany, Heinz Grieffenberger took over an ailing company in 1983 called ABM Baumiller, a maker of motors and gearboxes for cranes. What he found was a company making a few standard products for a large number of customers. He quickly replaced the entire production process in order to tailor his products to individual customer's needs. "I can switch production to a different product within seconds," he boasted to *Business Week.*

To be successful in the future, companies will have to learn to make their production processes as versatile as Toyota's without losing efficiency. FLEXcon, for example, prides itself on its ability to "tweak" its highly complex, volume-intensive coating process to supply custom-tailored orders of 200 yards when all other competitors demand 10 times the quantity for a minimum order. And FLEXcon has mastered this versatility without losing efficiency.

In the computer peripheral business, a rising star is Exabyte Corporation, which has developed an ingenious device that can increase the amount of information stored on computer disks. The company, started in 1987, has already grown from nothing to $170 million. Although the company's growth was based on an exclusive technology that gave it a monopoly in the marketplace, market fragmentation was at the root of its success. Its CEO, Peter Behrendt, said in an interview with *Planning Forum:* "Our customers wanted the product 'customized.' We had to set up a product in 100 different flavors; set up a manufacturing system rather than batching things, that at the end of the line produces the one the customer wants. We solved that problem."

Dell Computers is another example of a company that has changed the rules of marketing PCs not so much through the use of direct marketing methods but by practicing market fragmentation. It has achieved the ability to customize every PC ordered to each customer's individual needs by transforming its assembly process into one of the most flexible in the industry. Dell has simplified its product and component configurations into a made-to-order manufacturing operation by pushing customization to the end of production and transmitting order information to the shop floor every 24 hours. This has resulted to three- to four-day production and delivery cycles.

If Shaquille O'Neal (7-foot-1-inch, 310 pounds) wanted a bicycle, he couldn't walk into any store and buy one. Because of his size and weight he would require one made to measure. Until Cannondale Corp, of Georgetown, Connecticut, came along, that would have been an almost impossible task. However, for Cannondale, it is one day's work. Cannondale's manufacturing process is so versatile that it can handle such requests as reinforced tubes, larger wheels, larger and stronger seats and extended backs, in a normal workday without disturbing the remainder of its production for that day—and at premium prices. In yet another study of the future of manufacturing, conducted by *Management Review,* the conclusions were pretty much the same as ours. Here's their view of the future: "A woman peers at the image of a microwave oven on the personal computer in her home office. With the mouse on her PC, she selects from an array of options: size, color, digital display, rotating carousel. As she changes the specifications, the illustration represented on the screen changes. When she's satisfied with the results of her design, she 'modems' an order for the microwave to the manufacturer, bypassing the company's order department completely. Presto! Her 'personalized' microwave is manufactured that night and shipped the next morning."

The key to achieving such manufacturing prowess will be to *decentralize* and *delocatize* the manufacturing process. Two such companies have already done this. One is Eyelab, which has taken the manufacturing of lenses for glasses from a large, centralized factory to a multitude of small, decentralized ones each located in the back of the store where you buy your lens. Other, companies known as photofinishers, such as Moto-Foto, have done the same for the processing of film into finished photos. As a result, both these companies have shortened the turnaround time from a week to one hour.

Product versus Process Innovation

Under a push economy, when there is always a long line of waiting customers for your product, the type of innovation needed is usually that of product innovation. This is so because there are few competitors, and the occasional introduction of new product versions is enough to succeed.

In a pull economy, however, with multiple competitors, product innovation alone is not sufficient to succeed. Process innovation is now a required skill. Historically, the United States has not been very capable at process innovation compared to the Japanese and the Germans. And the reason can be found by looking at where each country's R & D money has been invested over the last 30 years:

	Product R&D, percent	Process R&D, percent
United States	70	30
Japan	30	70
Germany	50	50

Germany's balanced expenditure between product and process innovation probably explains why it has been even more successful than the Japanese since the end of World War II.

High versus Low Brand Loyalty

Another major effect of the pull economy and a contributor to the success of companies practicing market fragmentation is the change in the loyalty of consumers to traditional brands. In a push economy, there is strong brand loyalty because there is restriction of choice for the consumer and limited supply. As a result, the producer talks itself into believing that its products have strong brand following. In a pull economy, brand loyalty suffers and, faced with more choices of ever increasing quality, the consumer's loyalty is to himself or herself and not the producer.

A result of this shift is the current cry among advertising agencies for higher advertising budgets to regain brand loyalty. The trend will continue to be in the opposite direction. A major winner in this shift from diminishing brand loyalty will be the providers of private label brands whose sales have been on the upswing for several years at the expense of the traditional brands. One of our clients, Torbitt & Castleman, has built itself into a very successful private brand company by pursuing this very strategy.

Changing Rules versus Fixed Rules

Under a push economy, the rules of play are set by the producer and forced onto customers. As long as a push economy exists, the producer enforces those rules and thrives from them. Under a pull economy, not only are the rules set by the customer but they are constantly changing. As a result, market fragmentators are very nimble people constantly monitoring and adapting to the evolution of customer needs in order to find new opportunities to identify slightly different needs that will lead to slightly different products which will allow them to fragment the market even further and make it still more difficult for their competitors.

Once, as I was walking through one of Caterpillar's plants, I noticed a red tractor in one corner and a blue tractor in another. "Are those competitor tractors that you plan to strip down?" I asked. "No. They're ours," replied the vice president. "Some customers don't always want yellow."

Ten years ago this would have been heresy at Caterpillar. This company could do no wrong from 1925 to 1982. But then, in 1982, even mighty Caterpillar was hit by the pull economy. Fortunately, Caterpillar has recognized the change and is responding. Today, Caterpillar is customizing 70 percent of its machines to the needs of each individual customer.

As reported in *EuroBusiness*, the CEO of Matsushita has said, "In the future the mass market will be the individual." A company that already practices this concept is the Karsten Company in Phoenix. It has taken a substantial share of the golf club equipment market by applying the same principle of fragmentation. Whereas most companies create generic clubs to fit all sizes of players, Karsten customizes each set to each player's physical dimensions. As its advertisements state:

> We, at Karsten, have always designed and built PING golf clubs to each customer's individual specifications. Just send us your golf size, height, and fingertip-to-floor measurements. These measurements help us make certain that the lie of each club rests properly on the ground. The lie of each iron must also be in proper relation to the length of the shaft. This is why a golfer's height is taken into consideration.

When was the last time you were asked these questions when you bought a set of golf clubs?

Companies that do not learn to practice market fragmentation, even to the level of single customers, will be the dinosaurs of the decade.

10

The Ultimate Goal of New Product Creation: Changing the Rules of Play

The best competitive position to be in is to have no competition. That position can only be achieved by not playing the way your competitors play the game but rather by controlling the game by creating products and support services that change the rules in your favor.

Many theories have emerged over the years about how a company goes about growing at a competitor's expense. The obvious method is to duplicate the competitor's products and then attempt to out-market, out-sell, out-manufacture, and out-service these competitors. This is called *imitation strategy*. In our opinion, *imitation may be the finest form of flattery, but it is the worst form of strategy.*

All one is doing with this approach is entering a race with no finish line. One competitor surges ahead of the other for a short period only to be overtaken by another competitor for another period, to then regain the lead for another period, to. . . . I think you see what I mean. A race with no end—and no *winner!*

In fact, if there is to be a winner, it probably will be the competitor with the largest market share. In other words, the competitor that started the race in the first place is more than likely to have greater lasting power than the rest of the field in this type of game. It's somewhat akin to playing poker with someone who has 10 times the bankroll you have. He or she will eventually wear you out. We have come to discourage this concept of competition, especially if you are second, third, or fourth in the market.

Our experience has shown that if you are not the leader, *never play the game according to the rules the leader has set.* Otherwise, you are certain to lose! In other words, do not try to "out excel" the competitor in its areas of excellence or strategic capabilities. Playing by the rules set by the leader in an industry is certain death over time. The leader understands the rules better—it designed them. The leader can enforce them more effectively; it has more resources to do so. And the leader will crush you!

A better approach, in our view, is to create products that *change the rules of play.* By changing the rules of play, you *neutralize* and *paralyze* the leader. While the leader is temporarily immobilized and on the sidelines, you can make significant gains against that competitor.

Examples of Companies That Have Changed the Rules

One of the first companies to introduce a paper copier was 3M. But within a few years, 3M was out of the copier business. During our consulting work with 3M, we asked some of their executives to explain what had happened. 3M, they said, sold their machines to their customers. Xerox introduced its copiers and started *leasing* them to its customers. The 3M executives could not figure out how Xerox could make money leasing machines. All the equations they used on leasing as an option turned out red ink. Model after model, time after time. 3M could not bring itself to understand the leasing business. As a result they were paralyzed, sat on the sidelines, and watched as Xerox took the market away. Xerox had changed the rules of play!

In 1980, Xerox had 97 percent share of the worldwide copier market. In 1985, it had 13 percent. Why? Cannon came in and completely changed the rules of play. Instead of offering xerography technology, it introduced its own. Instead of offering big machines, it introduced small ones. Instead of selling through a direct sales force, like Xerox's, Cannon went through distributors. Instead of leasing the machines, it sold them outright. It took Xerox five years to decide to sell through distributors, and it took Xerox seven years to wean themselves off their leasing revenue stream. Eighty-four percentage market share points later!

Significant shifts in market share only occur by changing the rules of play on the leader, not by imitating the leader! Imitating the leader, or others in the industry, does not result in significant shifts in market share. The game is played between the 40-yard lines.

Up 10 yards back 5 yards. Up 5 yards, back 10 yards. In the media world, Ted Turner has built CNN into a major network by not playing according to the rules set by the three major networks—CBS, NBC, and ABC—none of which has had any significant shift in market share for 25 years—since the three have products and programs that imitate each other. Instead of using standard broadcast technology, Turner went with cable and satellite. Instead of going with a variety programming format, he went with an all-news format. Instead of staying domestic, he went international. Who has made more money in the last 10 years? Turner—by about $10 billion dollars!

A company that has had considerable success in a very mundane business over the last 20 years is Domino's Pizza. And most of that success was achieved by changing the rules of play. Thomas Monaghan, founder of Domino's, invented the concept of "guaranteed home delivery within 30 minutes." This guarantee was possible because of the development of a special envelope around the pizza to keep it warm during the delivery. As a result, Domino's has grown to several thousand outlets with almost no reply from its competitors.

In the stock brokerage business, Charles Schwab has grown a very successful business from scratch by also changing the rules to his advantage. The firm's net revenues have risen to over $500 million, and its stock price has gone from $7 to $33—by not doing what other brokers do. Schwab's personnel are on salary versus commission, they take calls 24 hours per day on three shifts versus a one-shift day for its competitors, and 20 percent of its business comes from an automated system rather than through direct phone contact with a broker. As a result, Schwab has challenged and changed the most important rule of the industry: Schwab's commission rates are less than half of the traditional houses!

In Europe, another upstart is making substantial gains at its competitor's expense by changing the rules of play. Martin Carver, CEO of Bandag, Inc.—a tire retreading company—decided that his business could not grow by emulating his competitors. Instead of working through Bandag's own distribution system, as it had done for decades, Carver dismantled the company in favor of a franchise system that costs each franchisee $150,000. Unlike its competitors, which insist that customers come to the retreader's shop, Bandag franchisees come to the customer's premises in specially designed $60,000 trucks filled with tires and equipment. Furthermore, the trucks are sent out after hours so that the customer's business is not interrupted. The result? Bandag's share has grown from 5 to 20 percent in Europe and now accounts for 18 percent of the company's total business, as compared to 5 percent in the 1980s.

In the health care business, another company is succeeding by changing the rules of play to its favor. Employee Benefit Plans (EBP) has grown at a rate of over 30 percent per year for the last eight years by not playing the game the same way the other players do. Instead of having its customers' companies manage their health care programs through the purchase of insurance from insurance companies, EBP shows its customers how to manage their health care programs themselves, without the need of the insurance company and at a lower cost. As a result, EBP is now a $250 million company and soon to be much larger.

JCB, a U.K. manufacturer of backhoe loaders, has seen its business grow from $200 million to over $1 billion also by changing the rules of play on its bigger heavy machinery competitors. JCB has achieved this by giving its potential customer a trial run with its machines. Not a small marketing risk considering that each machine is worth around $80,000. But this practice, unique to JCB, has increased its share of market from approximately 180 units a year to over 2500 units in 10 years.

In the cosmetics industry, Anita Roddick has seen her company— Body Shop International—grow from nothing to over $200 million of business annually by breaking all the rules that the larger companies play by. Instead of using expensive packaging, as its chief competitors do, Body Shop utilizes plain, nondescript material. In an industry that spends millions on advertising, Body Shop spends nothing. In an industry that sells primarily through drug and department stores, Body Shop sells through exclusive franchisees. Its growth is consistently in the double digits, and its net profit is over 30 percent of sales!

In yet another industry, steel, a group of upstarts are in the process of changing the rules of play and creating major headaches for the traditional giants such as U.S. Steel, Inland, and Armco. New entrants such as Nucor and Chaparral are using "minimills," which represent a complete rethink of the steel fabricating process. Instead of making steel from ore that requires expensive coke ovens and blast furnaces, the minimill employs less costly electric furnaces that melt down scrap metal. As one executive of Chaparral Steel said to *Fortune:* "We're Big Steel's worst nightmare, and we're not going away."

In the trucking industry, Don Schneider, CEO of Schneider National, has equipped each truck with a computer and a rotating antenna. This allows him to keep track of each truck's precise location at any time and to redirect the trucks to respond to clients' requests more rapidly than any competitor. Confronted with some dramatic changes facing the trucking industry—mainly deregulation—most other companies lowered rates in an attempt to keep customers. Schneider opted to find a unique way to respond more quickly to customer needs and to maintain price and margins by providing more value.

Another revolutionary is Marty Wygod, founder of Medco Containment Services. Wygod changed the rules of the retail drugstore business by providing companies with prescription drugs through the mail instead of through retail drugstores. The effect is a substantially lower per-unit cost for the customer. The result? Medco had such an impact that Merck decided to acquire it in order to guarantee a channel for its products.

Even Gillette, the inventor of the razor blade, has decided that the only way to grow its business again is to "change the playing field," as Colman Mockler, ex-CEO, stated to *Forbes*. After having followed the crowd during most of the 1980s by trying to sell disposable razors and not doing very well at it because of the commodity, low-price, low-margin, low-profit attributes of this approach, Gillette decided it "had to change the playing field. Gillette had to convince consumers to pay more for systems instead of buying cheap disposables." And thus, its introduction of the Sensor razor and blade system, which has been a phenomenal success even at $3.30 each versus a 40 cents disposable, not to mention the endless need for replacement blades at 70 cents apiece. In one swoop, Gillette went from a low-margin business to a high-margin business with an automatic multiplier to boot! It recently repeated this success with the introduction of a version made especially for female users.

Dell Computer is still another example. Instead of marketing computers through stores, as the rules of the industry would dictate, a brash 19-year-old Texan, Michael Dell, decided to market computers using direct-marketing techniques. The result: an $800 million company after only five years, one that is still going strong even during the recession of the early 1990s.

Dell is in the process of changing the marketing rules in Europe as well. After having been told by all the so-called marketing experts in Europe that Europeans would never buy computers through the mail, Dell decided to go ahead anyway. Guess what? Dell's business in Europe is fast approaching the $200 million mark. In fact, Dell's success is causing all the existing makers of PCs to rethink their approach to the marketing of their own products. The company that changed the rules may soon see its new rules become the industry standard, which shows that sometimes one can be so successful by changing the rules that an entire industry might feel threatened enough to convert to the new way of playing the game. Even Digital Equipment Corporation took the plunge into direct marketing of its latest line of PCs.

In the airline industry, the fastest growing and consistently most profitable company over the last 10 years is not one of the big three—American, United, or Delta—but Southwest. From nothing 10 years ago to $1.2 billion in 1991, it did this by not playing by the market leaders' rules. Unlike the big three, Southwest does not use a hub-and-spoke system, it flies point to point. Furthermore, it does not issue advance boarding cards, it does not serve meals, it does not take other carriers' tickets, and it does not transfer luggage to other carriers. It plays by its own rules, and it has the big three worried. As Robert Crandall, CEO of American, recently stated in a *Business Week* interview: "Southwest will be as big as we are." Why? Because by changing the rules, Southwest has the big three paralyzed. With the massive computer infrastructure the big three have built to gain an edge in their reservation systems, eliminating boarding passes to match Southwest doesn't remove any costs from the system. In other words, the big three are paralyzed and "on the sideline." During this paralysis, Southwest is making significant gains at their expense.

In the United Kingdom, an entrepreneur is in the midst of changing the rules about how books are marketed. Tim Waterstone, the founder of Waterstone Booksellers, has introduced the concept of bookstores with over 100,000 titles—compared to the W. H. Smith stores, which carry less than half that number. Furthermore, Waterstone's stores are open until 9 p.m. every night including Saturdays and Sundays, a practice unheard of in the United Kingdom. Since 1983, Waterstone Booksellers has grown to 85 stores and opened the first of several U.S. stores in 1991.

Eyelab is a good example of a company that has changed the rules of play in order to make significant gains at its competitors' expense. In order to reduce the waiting time for new eyeglasses, it transferred the manufacturing process from a single, centrally located laboratory to minilabs at each of its stores. Every Eyelab store has its own lenses, frames, grinding equipment, and technicians who can provide customers with eyeglasses within one hour instead of two weeks.

The late Sam Walton, the founder of Wal-Mart, succeeded in dethroning Sears as the largest retailer in the United States. In just 30 years, his company went from nothing to $67 billion in sales to displace Sears, which had been around much longer and enjoyed sales in the billions before Wal-Mart was even conceived. How did Walton do it? Simply by breaking all the rules that Sears had invented. For example, instead of periodic sales, Walton introduced the concept of everyday discount prices; instead of concentrating in large metropolitan areas, he built his stores in small towns that others scorned. By the time Sears woke up to the threat, Wal-Mart's momentum was unstoppable.

In the insurance industry, every major company avoids car insurance like a plague. Except a company called Progressive Insurance. Most companies avoid this market segment because of the incidence of risky drivers based on an evaluation of their past history of speeding tickets. Progressive is changing the rules of play in this arena by going after only the "nonstandard" drivers who have had three or more speeding tickets in five years. Why is it willing to undertake this risk when other companies are not? Progressive does it by leveraging what it considers to be its strategic capability—its proprietary database on nonstandard drivers. Says CEO Peter Lewis: "We feel that we are more knowledge-able about the economic effects of insuring non-standard drivers than most of our competitors. We believe that an accident is a more likely predictor of a future accident than is a ticket." This approach has made Progressive the tenth largest insurer in the country with 1993 revenues of $1.3 billion, a 25 percent increase over the previous year.

Sometimes, changing the rules of play puts an entire industry in jeopardy. Such is the case currently in the pharmaceutical industry. The giants—Merck, Hoffmann LaRoche, Bristol-Myers Squibb, Sandoz, Ciba-Geigy, and others—are being challenged by a number of upstarts such as Genentech, Genzyme, Immunex, and Amgen. What do these upstarts have in common? They have changed the rules of play in regard to the process of drug development. Whereas the traditional companies have their roots in chemistry, the challengers have their roots in biology. As *Fortune* reported:

> The conventional chemical approach which still dominates drug development at the big houses, relies on hit-or-miss screenings of thousands of compounds in hopes of finding one that has medici-nal properties. Only 1 out of 10,000 winds up on the market.
>
> By contrast, the biotech approach starts with substances the body already manufactures, either to heal directly or to act as signals that mobilize the response to an intruder. Biotech companies analyze the structure of these compounds, which are large protein mole-cules. Then they use genetic engineering to copy them. With the biotech approach a remarkable one of every ten possibilities has proved out.

Other advantages in the areas of costs, speed of development, and effectiveness have industry experts worried that the traditional approach will not match these new rules. Thus, they question the abili-ty of the conventional, chemically based companies to survive in the middle to long term.

In Japan, a market that many companies claim is closed to foreign firms, one company is doing spectacularly well by changing the rules of play. That company, Amway, has been growing at a rate of 30 per-cent per year since 1979 for a total of $1 billion, one-third of the company's total revenues. How has Amway done this? By bypassing Japan's vaunted, closed, and entrenched multitiered distribution system and going direct through a sales force of 1 million Japanese—one-tenth of that country's population—who sell product door-to-door. So much for those who claim the market is impenetrable.

ReMax is the last corporate example we will describe, although many more exist. In the real estate business, most sales are transacted by salespeople affiliated with large retail chains such as Coldwell Banker, Merrill Lynch, Prudential, and Century 21. Most small, independent brokers are being gobbled up by these giants of the industry—except for ReMax. ReMax is a chain of independent real estate salespeople who are in the top 10 percentile of the industry in terms of productivity, who pay their own rent, who do their own advertising, and who keep a larger share of their fees. ReMax is growing at twice the rate of the larger chains.

What Happens When You Play by Another's Rules?

To illustrate how dangerous it can be to play by rules set by a larger competitor, let me use the example of a French television network called La Cinq. La Cinq came into being after the French government loosened control of the media in 1986. It blossomed initially by providing a large dose of U.S. soap operas, something unheard of in France until then.

Unfortunately, the French government regulated the number of advertising minutes the network could sell, 7 per hour, which did not generate enough revenue for the network to break even. It needed to attract more viewers in an attempt to increase its rates to advertisers. In a desperate attempt to draw viewers from its larger competitor TF1, La Cinq's management decided to adopt TF1's formula of expensive, live variety shows. Unfortunately, viewers did not switch, and La Cinq stopped broadcasting on April 12, 1992.

Another similar example also comes from Europe, this time England. The victim is *Punch* magazine. From 1841 to 1988 *Punch* carved out a very profitable niche for itself by playing to its own rules. It built a strong following among mid-40, university-educated, upper-middle-class readers. Its winning formula was an editorial mixture of highly literate but outrageous humor.

In 1988, a new editor decided to change that strategy and start playing the game according to other competitors' rules. Noting that a number of new magazines had sprung up catering to a younger reader, the editorial mixture was changed to appeal to this group. Unfortunately, the other competitors knew the rules better. Not only did *Punch* not attract the younger reader, it soon saw its traditional readers abandon it in droves. In 1992, *Punch* closed its doors for good.

Playing the game according to the leader's rules can be deadly.

The Japanese Rule Book

One could even take this approach and apply it to the success of Japan over the last 30 years. Lee Iacocca has repeatedly pointed out to us that the Japanese "don't play according to the same rules." And he may be right. Alan Blinder, in a *Business Week* article entitled "There Are Capitalists, Then There Are the Japanese," has documented some of these differences. "Studying the Japanese economy," he notes, "has led me to a tentative conclusion: that market capitalism, Japanese-style, departs so much from conventional Western economic thought that it deserves to be considered a different system." He goes on to quote a high-level official of Japan's Ministry of International Trade and Industry who remarked: "We did the opposite of what American economists said. We violated all the rules." Some examples: Whereas, in the United States, the system is geared to serving the needs of consumers, the system in Japan is geared to serving the needs of the producers. In the United States, the consumer is best served by innovating and holding down costs; in Japan, the producer seeks growth to create employment as an integral part of nation building. Whereas cartels are thought of as being detrimental to healthy competition in the United States, cartels are encouraged in Japan. Whereas U.S. public companies make many decisions on the basis of short-term profits to enhance shareholder value, in Japan, decisions are rarely made on the basis of short-term results or shareholders' concerns. In the United States, close buyer-vendor relationships are discouraged; in Japan, it is a fundamental concept of their success at quality improvement. Alan Blinder goes on to illustrate a long list of other Japanese practices that are different from U.S. practices.

In a second study of Japanese business practices conducted by *Fortune* magazine, still another way of changing the rules of play was detected. This one deals with how the Japanese account for costs in the development of new products.

> Like its famed quality philosophy, Japan's cost-management system stands Western practice on its head. For example, American companies developing a new product typically design it first and then calculate the cost. If it's too high, the product goes back to the drawing board—or the company settles for a smaller profit. The

Japanese start with a target cost based on the price the market is most likely to accept. Then they direct designers and engineers to meet the target. [See Figure 10-1.]

The Japanese company that has had the greatest success by setting a new set of rules is Toyota. When Toyota entered the car business, its executives visited Ford's plants several times to study Henry Ford's concept for the mass production of automobiles. They concluded that it would not be in their best interest to play the game in this manner. As a result, they set out to completely reinvent the manufacturing

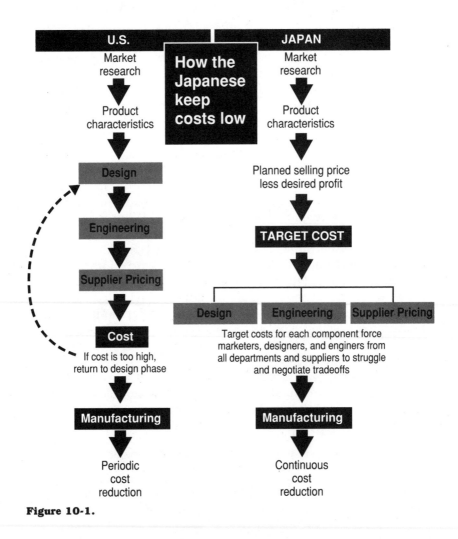

Figure 10-1.

process. This new process has since become known as the Toyota Production System and has not only contributed to Toyota's success but has since been copied by all Japanese companies and is probably the single most significant factor that has contributed to the dramatic rises we have seen in Japanese quality and productivity since the war.

American industrialists and politicians have spent inordinate amounts of time and effort trying to get the Japanese to play the game according to our rules. Instead they should recognize the fact that maybe—just maybe—the Japanese do not want to play according to our rules. After all, who's been winning the game? A better approach might be to spend time inventing a new game with new rules that are more to our advantage.

There is a blip on the horizon indicating that the United States may finally be catching on. The field is HDTV (high-definition television). For several years, a number of so-called experts made loud noises that if the U.S. government did not invest billions of dollars in the development of HDTV technology similar to that of the Japanese, the United States would lose control of the next generation of televisions and a potentially explosive growth market would revert again to the Japanese. Fortunately, nobody listened because copycatting the Japanese would have been doomed to failure.

Luckily for the United States, a company called General Instrument decided to change the rules of play and announced a *digital* HDTV! The Japanese system, based on an analog system, consisted of doubling the number of horizontal lines in order to produce better resolution. General Instrument decided that it had to tie its television to a world dominated by digital chips, digital compact disks, and digital telephones. Their system, based on digital technology, makes it easier to manipulate images, enlarge pictures, and even view images from different angles, not to mention what else will be possible as computer and telecommunication technologies continue to converge.

By refusing to play by Japanese rules and by creating new ones and tilting the field to its advantage, one company led the way to the U.S. reemergence as a powerhouse in the consumer electronics game.

The Moral of the Story

The moral of these examples is this: When you create new products with the intent to change the rules of play on the leader, you paralyze the leader, sometimes for long periods. The reason is simple. The leader's organization is structured to do business according to the rules it has set. Changing that structure is not easy and can sometimes take years. While the leader is immobilized, you can make significant and important gains.

The best way to make these inroads is to conduct your business using tactics that neutralize your competitor's most important strength. Think of ways that *circumvent* the leader's strength. In this manner, you can turn the leader's strength into a vulnerability. Trying to duplicate a competitor's key skill will put you in a race with no end. Run your own race!

This is what we find to be true in all the clients we work with. When everyone in an industry plays the game according to the same rules, no one wins! In other words, there are only marginal changes in market position. Those who make *significant gains at a competitors's expense are those who have found a way to tilt the playing field to their advantage* and change the rules of play.

After all, the object of competition is *not* to have an even playing field but to design a *playing field that is tilted to your advantage*, a playing field that paralyzes the competition. As General Sun Tzu would say, "To subdue the enemy without fighting is the acme of skill" (*The Art of War*, Second Abridged Edition, Shambhala, 1991).

The same concept applies to business. Do not play the game according to your competitor's rules. *Surprise* the enemy by changing the rules of play! If you are constantly being "surprised" by the enemy, this is a clear signal of a defensive, reactive strategy. Change it. A proactive product-innovation strategy constantly surprises the enemy and keeps the competitor in a defensive position!

11

Imbedding Innovative Thinking into the Fabric and Culture of the Organization

One of the interesting misconceptions that senior executives have about their job descriptions revolves around what it is they think that they manage. During my 20 years of consulting work with senior executives, I have often asked them: "What do you, as managers, 'manage'?" Their answer, 99 percent of the time, is "people."

"Not so," say I!

"Oh?" they reply.

"That's right!" I reaffirm.

"What then?" they ask.

"Here's what people in organizations really manage, " I reply.

Lower-lever people manage *things*. Middle managers manage *people*. Senior managers manage *processes*. In fact, one could view the hierarchy of management responsibility as shown in Figure 11-1.

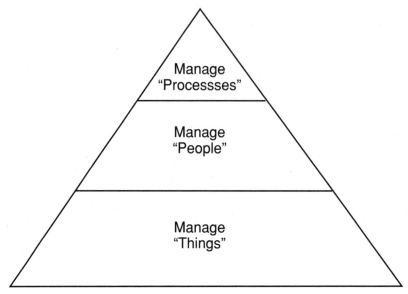

Figure 11-1. Hierarchy of management responsibility.

People Who Manage Things

These people are found at the bottom of the organization chart. They are the operators, mechanics, pipefitters, and electricians found in a manufacturing company, or the clerks and administrative personnel found in a white-collar area or in service industries. These people manage *things.* Their role is to get things done, to get the product out the door. Operators manage tools and production machines. Administrative people manage calculators, computers, or automatic teller machines (ATMs). They attempt to maintain these things in good working order in order to obtain the best yield and productivity from them.

People Who Manage People

These individuals are found in the middle of the pyramid. They are usually referred to as supervisors, foremen, superintendents in a manufacturing environment, or section heads, department chiefs, or even directors in a white-collar environment. They manage *people* because it is their role to schedule employees' time and shifts of work, handle their work loads, resolve their conflicts, and ensure that they are generally happy in their work. These middle managers are concerned about logistics, scheduling, and relationships.

People Who Manage Processes

These people reside at the zenith of the organization. Contrary to popular belief, these senior managers are not responsible for managing other people but rather for managing *processes.* Senior executives are responsible for choosing and putting into place the processes, systems, and/or methods that will get the people in an organization to behave as the organization wants. These systems include:

- Compensation
- Planning
- Budgeting
- Product development
- Test marketing
- Audit
- Promotion
- Performance review
- Job classification

I have often said to clients: "If you want to change the behavior of people, put it into the 'system.'"

To this list of "paper systems," our contention at DPI is that it is also management's responsibility to choose and put into place the *thinking processes* that they wish used in the organization. These are the processes of:

- Strategic thinking
- Innovative thinking
- Decision making

Building Innovative Thinking into the Organization's Culture

As I consult in various organizations, I am always told by the people of these organizations that "We have a different culture."

"What is your culture?" I ask.

"We cannot describe it," they reply, "but our culture is different than our competitors' or that of the company next door."

As a result of having heard these statements so frequently, I decided to investigate what it is about an organization that is at the root of that organization's culture. Studying organizations to uncover the answer to this mystery proved to be a futile exercise. To obtain an answer, we need instead to investigate what is at the root of the culture of a country. Then the answer becomes evident. The root of a country's culture is that country's language. Language is the root of literature, poetry, song, opera, music, theater, humor—all the elements that are *visible evidence* of a country's culture.

The analogy is this: *Language is to a country's culture what management processes are to an organization's culture.* Culture is the *result* of the *processes* that management chooses and uses to manage the organization.

Therefore, if management wants to create a certain culture in the organization, it must choose the processes that will cause its people to behave in a manner that results in the desired culture. The culture of an organization is the *result* of the processes with which management chooses to manage the business. This is so because a process provides a *common* language that can be used to deal more effectively with business issues. Just as language is the root of a country's music, literature, and theater, so is a common thinking process the root of better decisions, strategies, and new product and market opportunities for an organization.

If management wishes to breed a culture of sound strategic thinking, it must, thus, choose the process of strategic thinking that it wants its people to use. If management wishes to breed an innovative culture, then it must choose the process of product/market innovation it wants its people to use. In other words, management's role is to select the "languages" that it wishes its people to speak while conducting business on behalf of the organization.

Management's most important responsibility is to institutionalize these processes into the organization so that they become part and parcel of its fabric and culture. However, we have found that institutionalizing thinking processes into an organization is easier said than done. If one were to flowchart a business, the diagram would look like this:

Every business or organization can be broken down into three main components: (1) Every business takes certain raw materials (inputs), and (2) converts these (processes) into (3) a finished product (output).

Furthermore, everyone would agree that the *quality* and *quantity* of the output depends on the effectiveness of the process to convert the input into a finished product. In fact, the quality and quantity of the finished product is determined by the effectiveness of the process.

Tangible versus Intangible Processes

However, two kinds of processes exist in any business—tangible and intangible processes. The tangible processes are the obvious ones such as manufacturing, accounting, compensation, and capital expenditure (Figure 11-2).

The intangible processes are more subtle in nature but equally as important (Figure 11-3). These are the thinking processes that people use to manage the business and are the processes we have been discussing in this book. In business today, most executives are investing enormous amounts of money to improve their tangible processes and relatively nothing to improve the intangible ones. Our view is that the war will be won by the organizations who can outthink their competitors rather than those who can "outmuscle" them.

The difficulty lies in the fact that we are not dealing with a visible system such as a compensation scheme but rather with an invisible

TANGIBLE PROCESSES

Input (Raw Material)	Manufacturing	Output (Product)
	Invoicing	
	Recruiting	
	Marketing	

Figure 11-2.

INTANGIBLE THINKING PROCESSES

Input (Data)	Strategic Thinking	Output (Results)
	Innovative Thinking	
	Decision Making	

Figure 11-3.

process that occurs inside someone's head. The trick is to turn this invisible, uncoded, "soft" process into a codified, tangible tool that can be seen in "hard copy" form. As long as an organization's processes are uncodified and invisible, the organization will have difficulty perpetuating them and transmitting them to other people. If an organization wants to be successful, it must codify its key thinking processes in order to transfer them to large groups of people and ensure their use on an ongoing basis. Process implementation, then, becomes a critical subject, and will be discussed in the following chapter.

"How many such processes should we try to indoctrinate into our people?" you might ask. The answer is simple. Just as the best linguists can usually master only four or five languages, the same is true about management, or thinking, processes. No organization should attempt to use more than a few management processes if it expects its people to use and master them over time. The task of choosing thinking processes that are *critical* to the success of the organization is a key task of senior management.

12

Making New Product and New Market Creation a Repeatable Business Practice

As mentioned in a previous chapter, even well-intentioned companies do not have a systematic process to create, evaluate, develop, and pursue new market and/or new product opportunities. As a result, the process is conducted in a haphazard manner or, at best, is practiced by osmosis. As also mentioned in the previous chapter, any process that is critical to a company's future must be *codified* if it is to practiced consciously and repeatedly. The following are some useful techniques to make innovative thinking and new product/market creation a repeatable business practice.

Ban the Word *No*

In the work we do with our clients we frequently come across middle managers who tell us: "It's not that we lack new product opportunities that is a problem around here. The problem is simply that management turns everything down." In other words, management says no to everything that is proposed as a new product or new market concept.

The message that goes out to the organization is that management is not interested in new product/market opportunities, and the result is exactly that—middle management stops proposing them.

Upon a more careful analysis of this phenomenon, we have come to two interesting conclusions. We have not met a CEO, or a management team, that purposely attempts to discourage new product creation. We have also noticed, however, that when presented with new opportunities, they have no choice but to say no. The reason is simple. Management, through the use of very acute questions, can quickly pick the recommendation full of holes, and the proposal gets rejected or sent back for more work. This frequently happens because the proposers have not thought through the consequences, risks, or potential problems of their new concept. In other words, they have not considered the development nor the pursuit step of the process described in this book. No wonder management says no.

Indoctrinate All "Key" People in the Concepts and Process of New Product Innovation

As John Kotter pointed out in *The Leadership Factor* (Free Press, 1988), during peacetime, an army needs few leaders. However, during a time of war, it needs many. The same is true of new product innovation. When there is no competition, there is no need for new product innovators. With intense competition however, a company needs as many as it can deploy. Some companies attempt to delegate the development of new concepts to a small group of specialists or experts, mandating them to generate new product opportunities on behalf of the corporation. What these executives fail to realize is that creativity has no geography. Everyone involved in the new product creation "chain," including customers and suppliers, need to be indoctrinated in the concepts. New product/market creation needs to be delegated widely throughout an organization and not restricted to a small band of specialists.

The best leaders, in our view, can pass on, or teach, their skills to others. We cannot do this until we are fully conscious of the process or methods we use to achieve success. Good athletes usually do not make good coaches because while they were athletes they never analyzed the process or method that they were practicing and that made them successful. As a result, when they become coaches, athletes cannot develop these skills in anyone else because they cannot describe these skills. The best coaches, however, were not necessarily the best athletes but were, rather, "students of the game." These are the people who studied the methods or processes used by successful athletes; they discovered them and now can pass them on to others. A casual jogger does not necessarily pay much attention to the mechanics of jogging. However, if the jogger wishes to compete successfully in a marathon, he or she needs to become familiar with the technique, or *process*, of running in order to run in the most effective manner.

The same is true of product innovation. The process of innovative thinking can be studied and learned. To win against innovative competition, a company must master the process better than competitors do.

Develop a System to Collect New Product/Market Concepts

One of the most important realizations management must recognize is that any organization needs *two* management systems. One is used to run the existing business, and the second is used to run the *future* business. The first is dedicated to the management of current productors, current customers, and current markets. The second is dedicated to the development of concepts for future products, future customers, and future markets. And the two systems are different and need to be kept separate. The first is usually past-oriented and deals with problems and difficulties current products are encountering in current markets.

The second needs to be future-oriented and needs to deal with the creation of *future* products for *future* markets. Most organizations usually have sophisticated systems and formal forums and meetings to run the current business, but few have a formal process to create new product ideas and concepts. Managers are generally presented with problems, and they see their role as resolvers of problems. If that is their central identity and their basis for recognition, the chances are that they, and the organization, will never be very innovative. Reports that are produced in most organizations have a tendency to focus on negative deviations and underperformance. Such systems tend to breed problem solvers and not opportunity generators. Management vision, therefore, needs to be focused on opportunity and to be future-oriented. Opportunity creation, selection, and pursuit must be supported by formal structures and systems and managed apart from what's broken at this moment or from responding to competitive pressures, all activities that breed reactive behavior. As Peter Drucker wrote, "Resources, to produce results, must be allocated to opportunities rather than to problems."

Innovative thinking needs to breed proactive behavior. Management meetings, therefore, should have separate agendas that focus on opportunities as well as problems. Management's challenge, then, is to understand the *process* of new product/market creation and innovative thinking in order to *institutionalize* it as a formal activity in the organization.

Form a New Product Committee

One way to encourage the development of new product/market concepts is to have a standing committee that serves as a focal point to review and activate new concepts. Its mandate would not to be the *generator* of new product or new market concepts but rather the *assessor*, approver, initiator, and monitor of new opportunities.

Encourage Risk Taking

When I worked at Johnson & Johnson in the early 1960s, a motto permeated the organization: "If you're not making mistakes, you're not making decisions." Although I have been absent from J&J for over 30 years, I am convinced that motto still permeates the company. And the reason is simple—that is how J&J encourages risk taking. 3M does it in a similar fashion. "Make a lot of little mistakes, but try to avoid big ones" is 3M's way of doing the same thing. 3M further encourages risk taking through a concept it calls "bootlegging." People at 3M are allowed to dedicate 15 percent of their time to any project they wish without the approval of any of their superiors. Innovative thinking involves risk taking. Prudent and calculated risk taking, but nevertheless risk taking. None of these organizations, however, bet the house on one role of the dice.

For example, most people would consider Bell Laboratories to be one of the more conservative and prudent organizations that exist. Yet for the last 90 years starting with the design of the automatic telephone switchboard, to the development of the transistor, to the invention of semiconductors, to the development of optical fiber cables, Bell has produced a continuous stream of innovative winners. Obviously, Bell Labs has a process to assess relative risk versus potential benefit.

In many companies, certain management system discourage risk taking. An article in *The Academy of Management Executive* (February 1988) makes this point quite clearly:

Many market losses experienced by American firms can be attributed to a *lack of emphasis* on *product* and *process innovation*. *Product innovations* create new market opportunities, and in many industries are the driving force behind growth and profitability. *Process innovations* enable firms to produce existing products more efficiently. As such, process innovations are the main determinants of productivity growth. In this technologically dynamic era, without a continual stream of product and process innovations, firms soon lose their ability to compete effectively.

The author went on to point out that the United States's declining competitiveness is due to a decrease over the last five years in both product and process innovation compared to other countries such as Japan, West Germany, Italy, and even the United Kingdom. The author attributed the cause of this decline to the "quantitative" management systems espoused in the United States such as "ROI [return on investment]-based financial controls and portfolio management concepts." These principles, the author argued, "give rise to a short-term orientation and risk avoidance. . . . The argument to this point has been that reliance on tight financial controls by the corporate office encourages decision-making at the divisional level consistent with short-run profit maximization and risk avoidance. The result is lower innovative activity and declining competitiveness."

The risk-avoidance style of management in existence today in many U.S. companies has already cost the country dearly. Many inventions that were birthed in the United States have seen the light of day as innovative new products abroad. On example is the transistor, which was invented by Bell Laboratories but exploited by Sony of Japan. A second is the videocassette, which was invented by California-based Ampex but exploited by Sony and JVC.

Encourage Small as Well as Large Product Innovations

The message here is clear. Don't bet the future of the company on the ever elusive "eureka" project. Naturally, if a big bang comes along periodically, all the better. In the meantime, however, it is wise to promote marginal, incremental, but continuous product innovation. 3M was obviously very pleased by the enormous success of Post-it Notes. However, the dozens of new versions of masking tape, each one a "tweak," are just as important to 3M's success. The key is have a hopper full of new product concepts that can be opened at a moment's notice to allow another new concept to come to life.

Measure Innovation

As Peter Drucker has said: "If something is important to the organization, measure it!" We couldn't agree more. 3M, again, measures its new product development effort by mandating that every one of its 52 divisions produce 25 percent of its revenues from the introduction of new products every five years. Rubbermaid does it as well. Rubbermaid's mandate is that 33 percent of revenues come from products fewer than five years' old and, furthermore, that by the year 2000 that 25 percent of total revenues be from new markets outside the United States.

Reward and Compensate Innovation

I am a firm believer that, in business, people do not do what you want them to do but, rather, they do what you pay them to do! Therefore, if your people are not rewarded and compensated for their new product/market creation efforts, these efforts will not occur. Therefore, a must of any new product/market creation program is that there be in place a visible system of rewards with accompanying compensation.

Depending on the strategic thrust of the company, the reward system may need to be skewed to encourage different categories of innovation. If your survival is based on staying ahead of the pack, then *new-to-the-market* innovation may need to be compensated more than *product extensions.* If your strategy is to be a quick follower, then *new-to-us* innovation should be better rewarded. The key is that the compensation system of the corporation needs to encourage product innovation that supports the strategy of the business.

Test New Product Innovations Rigorously

Product innovation should be encouraged and rewarded but subject to the same disciplines and audit that any other request for funds and resources requires. Most companies test the justification of capital expenditure requests quite rigorously, but when it comes to doing the same for new product opportunities, they don't quite know where to begin.

The following is a list of questions that can be asked of those presenting a new opportunity to the organization:

New Opportunity Assessment Questions

- What is the *source* of this opportunity?

- How many other opportunities were considered?

- How did it rank in terms of cost/benefit? Strategic fit and difficulty of implementation?
- How did it rank in terms of risk/reward?
- What is the spread of risk/reward versus other opportunities?
- What are the *critical factors* that will cause success? Failure?
- How will you promote success? Avoid failure?
- What is your implementation plan?
- What do you think is the probability of success of your plan?
- Who will manage the plan?

These questions are the ones that the presenter and conceiver must ask of his or her own opportunity; these are the questions that management must responsibly ask and have answered to intelligently evaluate innovative opportunities. Since innovation is manageable, it should be subject to review and objective measurement, and the process is as important as the content.

Turning Product Innovation into a Reflex

A conscious management process needs to be institutionalized to become a repeatable business practice. In other words, over time the process should become a reflex. The notion of cascading these processes down the organization is also critical to the success of the organization. The reason is simple. Unlike what many think, it is the processes that management puts into place in the organization that will get people to behave in a certain manner. The dissemination of these fundamental processes throughout the organization is then vital to its success. The winning organization, in the long run, is not the one that can outmuscle its competitors with technical skills but rather the one that can outthink its opponents. Unfortunately, thinking is a rare skill in U.S. business today. The best companies have mastered the skills of innovative thinking and have the ability to instill these skills in the dozens, hundreds, or even thousands of people throughout the organization.

The process described in this book can make new product/market innovation happen on a continuous basis. The CEO's role is to provide a forum and a framework within which it can occur. This means conducting meetings (forums) in which part of the agenda is dedicated to searching for opportunities together with a formal process (framework) that makes it happen.

John Gardner, in his 1983 book *Self-Renewal* (Norton), said that to have renewal you need the seemingly exclusive conditions of stability and innovation, because stability without innovation is stagnation, while innovation without stability is anarchy. He argued that you need to have innovation in content and stability in process, and we concur.

13

Gillette and Kodak: Two Actual Sagas

The Gillette Saga

There is no better example of a company that has experienced and practiced the concepts described in this book than The Gillette Company. Founded in 1901 by King Camp Gillette, the inventor of the razor with a replaceable blade, the company came to dominate the industry, a position it held until 1980. That position had been built on its technological and marketing capabilities that resulted in a string of new product introductions all related to razors and blades.

Losing Sight of One's Strategic Capabilities

In the 1970s, however, a Gillette CEO lost sight of its *strategic heartbeat* and accompanying *areas of excellence* and the company embarked on a series of acquisitions that had nothing to do with razors and blades. The result was predictable. By 1986 the company's position had been so confused that it attracted no fewer than four corporate raiders in three years. The company had a sudden wake-up call.

Changing the Rules of Play

Under ex-CEO Colman Mockler and now under the current CEO Al Zeien, the company recognized that it had become hostage to the entry of disposable razors, which were taking any growth in the market with lower prices and causing the erosion of margins at Gillette. After trying to imitate the disposable products without much success, Gillette found itself at a crucial crossroads. One group within management emerged to promote the notion that razors had become commodity products and that the only way to play the game was on volume and low prices. A second group, however, felt that the company had allowed the products to become commodities since Gillette had "parked" its R&D program over the last 10 years and had allowed competitors to catch up. Luckily, this latter group won the debate.

In the selling of disposables, the key was massive and expensive investments in marketing, with total disregard for superior technology. A proposition was advanced by John Symons, then head of European operations, that customers would pay higher prices for superior technology. To prove his point, Symons decided to stop all advertising behind disposables and directed his marketing budget toward the support of "shaving systems" such as the Trac II and the Atra. Almost immediately, Gillette's growth rate accelerated in Europe and that of disposables slowed.

"It meant we had to change the playing field," said Symons "because Gillette had to convince consumers to pay more for systems instead of buying cheap disposables" ("We Had to Change the Playing Field," *Forbes*, February 4, 1991). The tactic worked. Sales of disposables dropped while sales of its higher-priced, higher-margin cartridges more than offset the shift. As a result, Gillette management decided to change the rules even more, and to do so around the world, by rededicating itself to new product creation that stemmed from its traditional prowess of technological innovation.

Breaking the Commodity Mindset

In order to break the commodity mindset, management decided to introduce a new product that had been conceived in 1979; Gillette poured $200 million to bring it to fruition. The new product was the Sensor. The Sensor was a quantum leap in razor technology. It had twin blades that floated on tiny springs and provided a closer shave than any other product available at the time of introduction.

"We saw this product (the Sensor) as the weapon to reverse the trend towards disposable razors," said CEO Alfred Zeien. The new product did cannibalize sales of the company's Trac II and Atra, but that was expected. What was unexpected was that the cannibalization of Gillette's older products was far less than what the company expected. Better yet, 14 percent of Sensor sales came from competitors' disposable products, about double the rate expected. The growth rate of disposables was stopped dead in its track, and the big losers were disposables by Schick and Bic. Over 35 million blade cartridges were shipped in the first year compared to the company's expectation of 20 million.

Fragmenting the Market

Historically, Gillette had tried to appeal to women by simply advertising its men's product to the female population without changing the product. With the enormous success of the Sensor, the company wanted to fragment the market between men and women and decided to conduct some research to see if women had dissimilar needs from men. The result was a resounding yes! Women did not like the narrow stem of the razor, which slipped out of their hand when used in a wet bathtub. Women also found it difficult to maneuver a man's razor on round surfaces or when bending to shave a leg. So the company introduced a revolutionary new product designed to address these two specific needs. The new product had a much broader handle that fit into the palm of a woman's hand more comfortably for use around the leg without the risk of slippage. Furthermore, it had a broad strip impregnated with aloe to leave a soft, satiny feel on the skin. The result? Today, sales of Sensor for Women are approximately the same in number of units as for men—well over 11 million per year—putting another dent in the disposable market.

Leveraging Strategic Capabilities across the Broadest Array of Products

Another concept that Gillette learned to use to its advantage was to leverage its strategic capabilities (areas of excellence) across the widest array of products. The Sensor for Women product has the same patented pivoting blade cartridge system as the men's product. Furthermore, both products have the same rubber grip developed for the pen's group Flexigrip pen.

Leveraging Strategic Capabilities across the Broadest Array of Markets

On the geographic front, Gillette is practicing both leveraging and fragmentation. Instead of imitating the current competitors which are already there with single-blade and single products, Gillette is conquering international markets by introducing multiple, double-blade products simultaneously. This approach both leverages Gillette's technological capability and fragments the market against its competitors.

Another tactic used by Gillette to conquer international markets is to immediately set up local manufacturing in order to satisfy local product and distribution more quickly than its competitors.

New Product Creation Provides Exclusivity

As mentioned in a previous chapter, one the advantages of *new-to-the-market* products is that they provide the company with the opportunity to build into the product some barriers to entry that make it difficult for competitors to duplicate the new product, providing the company with a period of exclusivity and premium prices. Such was the case with the Sensor; Gillette was able to incorporate 17 patents into the construction of the product which make it almost impossible for competitors to imitate it.

Making New Product Innovation a Repeatable Business Practice

Now that Gillette has experienced the positive effects of a strategy that promotes the continuous creation and introduction of new products, the company has decided to make it a repeatable business practice. Gillette has just announced the introduction of a new razor called the Sensor Excel which has new, additional features over the Sensor and which will be priced, naturally, at a higher price which will generate higher profits.

Gillette will continue to use technology and innovation as the best marketing tools and leave disposable and generic products to others. "Long term, innovation is really the thing that is going to separate the good from the superior," says Robert Murray, Gillette's executive vice president ("It's My Favorite Statistic," *Forbes*, September 12, 1994).

The Results

Since management's rededication to new product creation, the number of new products introduced has accelerated. In 1993, the company introduced 22 new products, and the number is expected to increase in 1994 and 1995. Over the last five years Gillette's sales have grown at an annual rate of 9 percent while earnings have grown at an annual rate of 17 percent. Total revenues have increased by 54 percent in the United States and 71 percent in Europe. As the saying goes, Gillette is on a roll.

The Kodak Saga

Kodak, another U.S. corporate superstar, is undergoing a metamorphosis similar to that of Gillette's. The only difference is that it is five years behind. Like Gillette, Kodak was founded in the late 1800s, by George Eastman who invented the first easy-to-use "consumer" camera and film. By the early 1900s the company was a worldwide powerhouse and maintained its dominant position until the 1970s. That's when the saga began.

The Sin of Mature Markets

After close to 90 years of market dominance, Kodak's management convinced itself in the early 1970s that its markets were maturing and that future growth would be difficult to find. As a result, Kodak went looking for opportunities outside the photography arena, and it made several acquisitions in the pharmaceutical area, an arena it knew nothing about and where Kodak's traditional strategic capabilities could not be leveraged. With Kodak's eye off the ball and with its resources deployed elsewhere, Fuji and 3M started eating away at Kodak's market share.

Worshipping at the Altar of the Cash Cow

Kodak then went on to multiply its strategic woes. The 1980s saw the advent of electronic photography, promoted initially by Sony, and Kodak's management aggravated its deteriorating position by trying to protect its cash cow. Recognizing the threat that electronic images represented to the more conventional "paper" images, Kodak delayed entering this field for the fear that electronic photography products would cannibalize Kodak's conventional ones. The effect: paralysis and an accelerated decline. By 1993, after five restructurings that eliminated 40,000 jobs, Kodak was in intensive care.

Rededication to Its Strategic Capabilities

In 1993, Kodak's board finally acted and, in December, appointed George Fisher of Motorola its new CEO. Fisher wasted no time in deciding where Kodak's future lay, and that was not in pharmaceuticals. Within a matter of weeks he sold off all these unwanted businesses and ended up eliminating all the company's debt of $6.3 billion; he even ended up with $1.3 billion in cash to invest. In what you might ask? Photography, naturally.

Breaking the Mature Market Mindset

Fisher took a look at one statistic and convinced himself that the market was a long way from being mature: "Half the world has yet to take a picture," he says.

Creating Products for the Future, Not the Present

To rejuvenate Kodak's creative juices, Fisher has been going around the Kodak empire urging employees to rethink photography and photographic products. "People put pictures in drawers or photo albums," he tells them. "We have got to get them on to networks." He then describes the future. "I think one day I'll pull out my small handheld computer, go through my pictures and transmit a few to my parents, who will put them on a thermal printer." Kodak's new CEO is deliberately attempting to focus the company's product innovation grey matter toward the creation of new-to-the-market products and not product extensions.

Leveraging Strategic Capabilities

Unlike Kodak's previous management, Fisher does not see electronics as a threat but rather as a natural extension of the company's strategic capabilities: "I feel viscerally that we're on the verge of a major revolution in getting high quality images on to information networks. Kodak is the best positioned company to achieve that" ("A New Picture at Kodak," *U.S. News & World Report*, September 19, 1994).

The next few years will interesting ones for Kodak watchers. Will Kodak go the way of Borden or will it revitalize itself like Gillette did? Stay tuned.

14

The Tangible and Intangible Outputs of the Process

Like any marketer of any product, we periodically survey our clients to verify that they are getting the results they expected from the use of our product-innovation process. Like any marketer of any product, we discovered that the process has delivered some expected results but that is has also delivered some unexpected, but highly welcomed, outputs as well. These results seem to fall in two categories: tangible and intangible.

The Tangible Results

The *tangible* outcomes are the ones that are expected, since these are the outputs the process was designed to produce.

The Search Outputs

The search step provokes the company to explore every nook and cranny of the business and its environment, to lift every rug to find any change that can be converted into an opportunity for a new product, customer, or market. The tangible outcome of this step is an ongoing inventory and hopper full of new product/market concepts that are available to the organization at any point in time.

The Assessment Outputs

The second step in the process helps the company evaluate all the concepts and opportunities and rank them in terms of potential for the company. The tangible outcome after this step is a list of specific new product/market concepts ranked in order of potential merit.

The Development Outputs

The third step in the process starts orienting management's thinking toward the critical factors that will cause the eventual success or failure or each new opportunity. This step also brings in the risk/reward filter, which helps the organization focus on "la crème de la crème" of new product/market concepts. The tangible outcome is a short list of the very best opportunities available to the company.

The Pursuit Outputs

The last step in the process bridges the transition from thinking to action. This pursuit step obliges management to anticipate the critical factors that would cause success or failure and to design an implementation plan that incorporates actions to prevent failure and other specific actions to promote success. Furthermore, each step of the plan is assigned to a specific person whose responsibility will be to complete that step in full and on time. The final outcome is a concrete implementation plan for each of the high-potential opportunities that have passed all the previous filters.

The Intangible Results

While we were working with several clients which provided us with opportunities to test our new product innovation concepts and as we were developing and refining these concepts, we always went back to ask these clients if the results described above had occurred. "Yes," they said, "but a lot of other good things have occurred as well." They then went on to describe a number of outputs that were more *intangible* in nature but, to them, seemed as important as the tangible ones.

A Perpetual Inventory

The first such result they spoke about was that the process had produced a large number of new product/market concepts. Starting with a bare cupboard, each company now had an abundance of new opportunities that it could capitalize on. Furthermore, the cupboard could be replenished at will by simply reusing the process whenever enough changes in the business environment justified so doing.

Proactive versus Reactive

Because most companies did not have a systematic method to create new products or markets, they would do so as reactions to competitive moves rather than at their own initiative. Using our process consciously, they said, caused them to turn their product development program into a proactive one that they controlled.

Pacing

Because the search steps produce an abundance of new concepts, the company is now in a position to pick and choose the opportunities it wishes to pursue and to do so at a pace it chooses rather than be at the mercy of competitive forces. Intel is a good example of a company that has mastered this concept. Intel introduces new products when it chooses to do so and not when its competitors dictate.

From Subjectivity to Objectivity

Many clients told us that the process, especially the assessment step, brings objectivity to what can be a very subjective topic. This is particularly true when a company attempts to rank opportunities in terms of potential to the organization. Because each person has certain inbuilt biases for a particular opportunity and against another, this exercise can turn into an emotional free-for-all. The assessment step brings to that discussion an objective template that subdues emotional data and substitutes rational evaluation factors and criteria.

Common Language

Every client mentioned that, for those who had participated in the work sessions, the process gave them access to key terms and concepts that became a common language used by them after the session. In other words, the process provided a glossary of key words that facilitated communication between these people whenever they met to discuss new product/market opportunities.

Consensus

Everyone mentioned the process's ability to breed consensus among individuals who had very differing opinions about what the company should create and how to pursue new opportunities. They stated that in a systematic, step-by-step manner conclusions are reached at each step, thus building consensus along the way. Furthermore, because everyone has had a chance to state her or his views about each opportunity taken through the process, the resulting opportunities are the construct of the entire team and not just one individual's "brilliant" idea.

Repeatable Business Practice

Client after client, to our surprise, had taken all or pieces of the process and had institutionalized it as an ongoing practice in the business. The benefit, clients said, was to turn the practice of new product/market creation from a haphazard, slipshod occurrence into that of a systematic, organized approach that is practiced visibly and consciously rather than by osmosis.

Index

About the Author

Michel Robert is founder and president of Decision Processes International, Inc., an internationally renowned consulting firm with 60 partners in 15 countries that is headquartered in Westport, Connecticut. His clients include such major companies as Caterpillar, 3M, Honda, GATX, and Johnson & Johnson. His previous books include the best-selling *Strategy Pure and Simple* (McGraw-Hill, 1993), which continues to have an impact upon many thousands of readers and hundreds of corporations each year.